Helping Your Child to Learn

Helping Your Child to Learn

A Proven System That Shows Parents
How to Help Their Children
Study and Receive Top Grades
in Elementary and Junior High School

Gordon W. Green, Jr., Ph.D.

A Citadel Press Book
Published by Carol Publishing Group

A Citadel Press Book
Published by Carol Publishing Group
Citadel Press is a registered trademark of Carol Communications, Inc.
Editorial Offices: 600 Madison Avenue, New York, N.Y. 10022
Sales and Distribution Offices: 120 Enterprise Avenue, Secaucus, N.J. 07094
In Canada: Canadian Manda Group, P.O. Box 920, Station U, Toronto,
    Ontario M8Z 5P9
Queries regarding rights and permissions should be addressed to Carol
    Publishing Group, 600 Madison Avenue, New York, N.Y. 10022

Carol Publishing Group books are available at special discounts for bulk
purchases, for sales promotion, fund-raising, or educational purposes.
Special editions can be created to specifications. For details, contact:
Special Sales Department, Carol Publishing Group, 120 Enterprise Avenue,
Secaucus, N.J. 07094

Manufactured in the United States of America
10 9 8 7 6 5 4 3 2 1

Library of Congress Cataloging-in-Publication Data

Green, Gordon W.
    Helping your child to learn / Gordon W. Green, Jr.
        p.   cm.
    "A Citadel Press Book."
    ISBN 0-8065-1497-3 (pbk.)
    1. Study skills. 2. Education—Parent participation. I. Title.
LB1049.G7295   1994
371.3'078—dc20   93-40569
                                                                CIP

In memory of my father
GORDON WOODROW GREEN, SR. (1923–1992)
who was my first and most influential teacher

Contents

Part Four
Making the System Work for Your Child

Foreword

After I wrote *Getting Straight A's*, many parents told me that a similar book was needed for their younger children who were experiencing difficulty in school. They said they did not know what they could do to help them. They also recognized that it is easier for older students to excel if they have been using proper study habits all along.

Helping Your Child to Learn is intended to fill this void. It covers everything that you as a parent need to know to help your child have a happy and successful school experience. *Getting Straight A's* was addressed to college and high-school students. The present book is geared to the needs of elementary and junior-high-school students. I direct my remarks to you the parent rather than the child, because parents are their children's most important partners in education. You are with your child from birth, and you play a major role in his or her physical, social, and intellectual development. *Helping Your Child to Learn* offers a methodical approach so parents can assist their children in becoming effective learners from their earliest years and enable them to make a smooth transition to becoming excellent students later on.

As parent and teacher you can help create the right environment at home to encourage learning. I start with things you can do when your children are at the earliest stages of learning, right from the point when they first begin to walk and talk. I present learning techniques that you can use as they progress through preschool, elementary school, and junior-high school. The discussion covers not only formal training in the classroom, but also things you can do to turn everyday occurrences into learning experiences that will transfer to the classroom. Since every child is unique and has his or her own best way of learning, I show you how to adapt the approach to meet your own child's special needs.

Many innovations have been tried in education in recent years, but educators continually tell us that we need to get back to basics. In this book I will show how you can help your children master the three R's: reading, writing, and arithmetic. Why are these basic skills so important? They are important because they are needed in practically every discipline children will study during their education. Every course has reading assignments in which students are required not only to read the material, but to understand the concepts presented to master a subject. Writing is the way they express themselves and demonstrate what they have learned, not just in English class but in all of their classes. And mathematics is required in all quantitative and scientific classes; indeed, many people will tell you that the mathematics makes these subjects difficult. There are effective ways to develop mastery of these basic skills from the earliest ages, and that is what I will be covering here.

The heart of this book is the presentation of a system that will show your child how to get good grades. Here I have adapted the proven techniques of *Getting Straight A's*, which have worked for hundreds of thousands of older students, to the needs of younger students. You will learn how to help children plan a course of study, so they will be motivated to work toward achieving a specific goal. I will show you how to work effectively with school teachers and administrators, so that you will become partners in developing your child's educational abilities. You will learn how to position your child for effective learning with basic tips on attending class regularly, sitting in the best spot, and completing assignments when they are due.

On a higher level, you will learn how to help your child develop skills that will be important later on, such as learning to take notes, mastering material presented in class, and preparing for exams. I will also show you how to help children gain proficiency in taking different types of tests, so they will view examinations as learning devices and not instruments of torture.

As their children's partners in learning, parents play a critical role in forming their attitudes about education and in helping them to achieve their goals. There is so much that parents can do in becoming good role models and providing an environment that is conducive to learning. I will give you numerous tips on how you can help children study effectively—by motivating them to work hard, instilling discipline so they will do what is required, and providing help that develops their abilities to do even more in the future.

There are many advantages in following these methods. You will have a child who is motivated to learn because he or she enjoys learning. As children become more proficient students, they set even higher standards for themselves. I have seen over and over again when children convince themselves that they can do the work of an A-student, they start thinking of themselves as A-students and are no longer satisfied with a lesser accomplishment. This makes it easier to develop a good foundation so they can become excellent students. Furthermore, you will raise a happy child who will have a much greater chance of succeeding in life. As one parent once said to me, "A successful student increases the quality of your own life!"

—Gordon W. Green, Jr., Ph.D.

Acknowledgments

Several individuals played important roles in the development of this book. First and foremost, I would like to thank Harold Roth, my literary agent, who has provided excellent advice over the years on topics for books and has helped to get them published. I have benefited from the careful instruction of teachers during my numerous years of being in school, and their wisdom is surely reflected here. My own three children, Heidi, Dana, and Christopher, have shared their experiences with me during their elementary and junior-high-school years, and their respective teachers have also had a significant influence on my thinking. I have also learned much from the many students who have used my study methods and communicated their experiences to me. My own parents, Gordon and Marie Green, practiced many of the techniques discussed here, and certainly have had a profound influence on my intellectual development. And last, but not least, I would like to thank my dear wife, Maureen, who typed the manuscript for this book. She not only grants me the time to write books, but keeps me moving at a rapid pace so I can meet my deadlines.

As surely as you are your child's first and most influential teacher, your child's ideas about education and its significance begin with you. You must be a *living* example of what you expect your children to honor and to emulate. Moreover, you bear a responsibility to participate actively in your child's education.

—National Commission
on Excellence in Education

PART ONE

THE IMPORTANCE OF YOUR CHILD'S EDUCATION

1

Introduction

The most important gift you have given your child is life. The next most important gift you can provide is a good education, because without a good education your child will have a hard time living a good life.

I am sure that all parents have told their offspring about the importance of education. We have made it clear to our children that they need a good education so they can get an interesting and challenging job, earn a lot of money, and live well. We probably have also told them that without a decent education they may have difficulty obtaining *any* job, will likely not earn very much money, and may have trouble making ends meet for the rest of their lives. We also made clear that they need to learn so they will have a fuller understanding of the world and what life is all about.

We tell our children these things not once, but over and over again, because they seem to have difficulty understanding them. This should not surprise us, because as parents we have the perspective that comes with living many more years than our youngsters. In addition, when we talk about education our children know that this usually means they must study when there are probably a lot of other things they would rather do. Sometimes our words seem to fall on deaf ears, but we persist in our

3

efforts because we know these things to be true, and because we care more about our children than anything else. Our efforts are very wise because the children we love so much are not just the future of our own family line, but of the nation and the world.

At the risk of saying some things you already know, let me quantify some of the factors I am talking about. Before becoming chief of the Governments Division at the U.S. Bureau of the Census, I spent almost two decades directing the preparation of statistics on income, poverty, labor force, and wealth. My Ph.D. in economics was based on income differences between men and women and blacks and whites in the labor force. These experiences have convinced me of the significant influence that education has on income levels.

The close association between education and income is apparent in the statistics. Based on a 1992 survey, men working year-round full-time with four years of college had average annual earnings of $44,540, about 58 percent higher than the average for high-school graduates, who earned $28,230. Women working year-round full-time with four years of college had average annual earnings of $30,000, about 55 percent higher than the average for high school graduates, who earned $19,340.

What is true for a single year becomes even more pronounced over a lifetime. Men working year-round full-time who are college graduates earn about $2 million over their lifetime compared with $1.4 million for men who are high-school graduates. The comparable figures for women working year-round full-time are $1.2 million for college students and about $870,000 for high-school graduates. Mention some of these numbers to your youngsters the next time you want to convince them of the importance of a college education—and then give them an idea of the kinds of things they can buy with the additional amounts of money. It's a very powerful motivator.

The importance of education will be much more significant for our children than it was for our generation. Recent statistics tell us that the income gap is growing even wider between highly educated and lesser educated people. The nature of work is changing dramatically as the world becomes a global marketplace. Routine work requiring fewer skills is moving to other countries that have relatively low wage levels. Jobs in the United States are becoming more specialized and require knowledge of advanced technology. These trends are expected to continue in the future. People who have high levels of education should benefit from the changing nature of work, while those with little education will lose out.

When our children apply for tomorrow's jobs, they will need every advantage they can get. They will be much more likely to obtain the good jobs and succeed in them if they have acquired high levels of education and have done well in the process. Employers do not consider only the level of education a person has attained. They also look for indicators like good grades—because good grades indicate that a person is mentally sharp, disciplined, and trainable. Workers in the future will require these qualities because their employers will face increased competition in the global marketplace, and advancing technology will require continuous training.

It is not enough for us, as parents, to tell our children that they need good grades now so they can get into a good college, get a good job, and have plenty of income to meet future needs. We need to go further by showing them the means to master their studies and obtain high grades. We need to do this as a partner in education because we play such a large role in our children's social, physical, and intellectual development. Do not think for a minute that you as a parent can sit back and merely advise your child on the proper course of action. Success will require that you participate actively and extensively in your child's development, starting from the earliest years, continuing up to the time when they are capable of self-reliance.

In *Helping Your Child to Learn*, I have distilled everything I know about the subject of education. In order to give you a better idea of what went into this book, and why the methods presented here are so successful, I will devote some space to describing my own background in the field of education.

I know a lot about students with problems because I was one of them. As a youngster going through elementary school, junior high, and high school, I was about as hard-headed as they come. My parents always emphasized the importance of getting top grades, but I was too busy playing sports and running around with my friends. Sound familiar? As a result, when I applied for college, the only school that would accept me was the state-run University of Maryland, which was required to admit all state residents at the time. The university insisted that I attend remedial courses in English and mathematics because of my poor grades. A few years passed before I settled down and started to do well in college.

After graduating, I worked for the federal government. Gradually I realized that going to college was a wonderful experience, so I decided to go back and take additional classes in the evening. At first I studied mathematics and statistics, but eventually I settled into a Ph.D. program in economics at the George Washington University. The experience proved especially worthwhile since I could apply much of my newly acquired knowledge to my work. I have remained with the federal government over the years and, as noted earlier, I am now chief of the Governments Division at the U.S. Bureau of the Census. In this capacity, I am responsible for directing the collection of a wide range of educational statistics from elementary, secondary, and postsecondary schools across the country. These various experiences have enhanced my ideas about education.

In the process of acquiring a Ph.D. in economics, I managed to get an A on every test in every graduate course I took. During these years I worked full time while I took care of my family and home. This accomplishment did not mean that I was a genius. My earlier grades already disproved that! Rather it meant I had developed a foolproof method of study, one that would work for students in any given situation studying any particular discipline. My first book, titled *Getting Straight A's*, described the learning methods that I had developed. Since it was first published in 1985, it has gone through numerous printings, been advertised repeatedly in *Parade* magazine, and sold hundreds of thousands of copies. The book is still available, in an updated edition, and has been translated into Spanish as *Como Sacar Una A*. Over the years I have received a huge number of letters and telephone calls from students, parents, and educators, which have confirmed over and over again that these methods really do work. Some of the students even send me their report cards.

In *Helping Your Child to Learn*, I have adapted these same study methods to apply to younger students. As a parent who has had children in elementary, junior high, high school, and college, at various stages of my life, I have a good appreciation of what is required at each level. This book is addressed specifically to the parents of elementary and junior-high-school students. It is my philosophy that students in these earlier grades should be learning and practicing the basic study methods they will use later on. In this way they will develop skills and a comfort level that will enable them to make a smooth and orderly transition to high school and college. The approach is analogous to developing ability in any sport that requires finely tuned skills, such as tennis, skiing, billiards, etc.—the object is to show students the proper methods early on so they will have a good foundation for developing more advanced skills as they grow older.

As a preview of what is to come in this book, I will give you some specific examples of how I have adapted these study methods. In my book for older students I devoted an entire section to mastering basic skills such as how to read a book, how to take a test, and how to write a term paper. It should be clear that a prerequisite for mastering these basic skills is an understanding of the three R's: reading, writing, and arithmetic. Thus, I have included a separate section in this book to show parents how they can help their children master these fundamentals.

In my opinion, everything starts with reading, so the often used phrase, "Reading Is Fundamental," is right on the mark. Reading is the mechanism that we all use to learn concepts and information. In addition to speaking and listening, it is one of the principal ways that we develop a vocabulary, learn about the world, and develop thinking abilities. There are certain things that we as parents can do to develop our children's reading abilities from the earliest years. This process starts with the simple fairy tales and stories that we read to them even before they know the meaning of the words we are using. It continues as we take them to the library and introduce them to new reading materials that catch their fancy and encourage them to read even more. And it is refined as we help them to understand the new words and concepts they strive to master in their formal studies. There are techniques that we can use not only to generate interest, but to help our children become more proficient and critical readers at the same time. I will cover these and other topics in the section on reading.

Writing is a more advanced skill than reading because we are expressing our own thoughts to others. Mastery of reading is a good precursor of writing because it familiarizes us with the approaches that others use to express themselves. Even if your child does not become a professional author, he or she will be required to write many essays and papers. Written work is the principal means that educators will use to assess how much your child has learned. Being able to think clearly is a necessary starting point for good writing, but there are numerous rules of grammar and mechanics of sentence and paragraph construction that one must master as well. The classroom is not the only place where one learns to write. There are numerous things that parents can do to help develop their children's ability at an early age. Being able to encourage children to write is the starting point, and helping them to critique and refine what they have written comes later. The rules of good writing are simple—not complex—and they can be taught by every parent. I will be teaching these rules to you in the section on writing.

In our increasingly complex and technological world, mastery of mathematics is becoming a necessity. Maybe there was a time when it was sufficient to know only how to add, subtract, multiply, and divide, in order to meet the basic requirements of daily living, but those days are rapidly disappearing. In today's world, people need knowledge of advanced mathematics to gain entry into well-paying fields in business and the sciences. You have probably discovered that your child is introduced to more advanced mathematical concepts in school earlier than you were. Many people, children and adults alike, have an absolute terror of mathematics known as "math anxiety." This comes mainly from not mastering the basics of mathematics at an early age. Mathematics is a very logical discipline that builds on past knowledge. Learning mathematics is like learning how to walk up a flight of stairs: everything is fine as long as you take one step at a time, but trying to leap over several steps at once can be disastrous. There are several things that parents can do to generate an interest in mathematics and nurture an aptitude if it is already there. I am in the process of writing a book on mathematics, and I will draw on this material for the section on arithmetic.

The centerpiece of my study book for older students is a system that shows students how to master their studies and receive the highest grades in their classes. Even many older students have not learned the proper methods of study because they have never been taught these methods in the classroom. Since many of these students do not know how to study, they do not study enough or they waste their time on what they do study. I firmly believe that a methodical approach shows students exactly what and how much to study. In this way they experience some success, which further motivates them, and good study methods become routine rather than a chore. My system of study is also the centerpiece of this book, but I have adapted it to apply to younger students in elementary and junior high school. In this way parents, the children's most important partners in learning, can help them master the proper study methods from the earliest grades so they can enjoy success now and later on.

Certain basic considerations apply to all students, regardless of grade level. Just as I encourage older students to think about what they want to do with their lives, and to plan a course of study toward that end, it is helpful to get younger students to begin to think the same way. There are things that parents can do to help their children understand different types of work, and to make them aware of requirements for entry for later schooling. Children who really want to be doctors or lawyers will be more motivated when they realize that they need good grades to get into medical or law school. Don't underestimate the importance of motivation in a young child. In a book I wrote titled *Getting Ahead at Work*, some of the most successful subjects knew what they wanted to be from a very early age. They also had parents who motivated them to work hard to achieve their goals.

Students must also learn to work well with teachers, attend class regularly, and sit in a location that facilitates learning. Parents have a responsibility to develop a sense of respect in their children for teachers, who are the other important partners in learning. How well your child does in school is measured largely by teachers' assessments.

In high school or college the teacher assumes that students have completed their assignments before coming to class, and that they know how to take careful notes to master the material presented to them. The teacher also assumes that students will do these things on their own volition. In turn, the students know the teacher will give them tests on the material that will determine their grade. Yet I do not have to tell you many older students fail to carry out their assignments. Many never learned how to study properly when they were younger. There are approaches that parents can use to show their children how to take notes effectively, master the material presented in class, prepare for and score high on exams. These are some of the other topics I will cover as I show you how to teach your children my student methods.

The role of parents in the educational process is similar to that of athletic coaches. Just as athletes need continual coaching on the proper methods of participating in their sport, students need continual coaching on the proper methods of studying. This means that you should not only learn the methods of study I will cover, you should help your child master these techniques. Telling your youngster what to do is not enough. A baseball coach can explain to a young player how to hit a baseball, but it will take a lot of practice and persistent coaching to eliminate the errors. Studying is no different. Parents will need to be there to give their children guidance and correct their mistakes. I am not recommending that parents do the work for their children, because this will prevent students from learning on their own and they will never gain self-sufficiency. The key is giving good advice at critical junctures so students can build a strong foundation for academic growth.

Parents should not only show their children how to study, they should also motivate them and create an environment conducive to study. The starting point is for parents to let their children know that they think school is important and that they genuinely care how their children are doing in their studies. Despite the rebellious attitude of many children, they really do care what their parents think and they want to please them. It is important for parents to send consistent signals to children. If parents say that school is very important—and really mean it—then children will think the same way. If parents say disparaging things about teachers and educational institutions, then they should not be surprised to hear their children saying the same things. I will show you how to be a role model for your children in a way that endorses a high regard for education and makes them want to study.

In everything that follows, I cannot emphasize strongly enough that you will have to be an active participant in your child's education. It won't do to stand on the sideline and observe. In *Helping Your Child to Learn*, I meant to emphasize the first word, *Helping*. If you are not willing to put in the time and effort required, then what I have to say will be little more than an academic exercise. You should follow the advice of the National Commission on Excellence in Education:

PRINCIPLE 1
You bear a responsibility to participate actively in your child's education.

2

Setting the Stage

Do you know why the National Commission on Excellence in Education referred to parents as their children's "first and most influential teacher"? Think of the following. You are with your child from birth, and yours is the face your child sees every night when he or she comes home from school. Your words and thoughts are what your children hear when they are with you. They seek to imitate your actions. You play a major role in their intellectual, emotional, and social development. Many teachers will also play a significant role, but they come and go with the passing of the years. In sum, *you* are the one source of continuity in your child's life.

Most parents naturally do certain things that stimulate their children's development. They provide love, nourishment, a secure environment, and intellectual encouragement, including play and answering simple questions. There are a number of other things that parents should do at each stage of their children's development that do not require much more time and effort than they are expending already. In order to describe these activities, I will divide the discussion into different stages associated with a child's development.

The Preschool Years

The preschool years begin with the first moment your child enters the world. Even though he or she is thrust into a new and foreign environment, with little more than inherited genetic traits, your baby is programmed to learn from the very start. Although newborn infants cannot yet see clearly, do not know a language, and have little control over physical movements, they will use every resource within their command to learn. Unlike the intellectual and abstract development that will come later on, your child employs the basic senses—sight, touch, smell, sound, and taste—to understand the world. He or she tries to comprehend the immediate environment and the animated forces that inhabit it—like you and other human beings. Parents are the most available and continuing presence in most infants' lives, and a significant bonding with them takes place shortly after birth. Children sense very early that a parent is a loving companion who will diligently look after their welfare and protect them. An added challenge is for parents to communicate early on to their children that they are also companions in learning.

As infants seek to understand the world, they hold, touch, smell, and see objects you put in and around the crib. As a general rule, bright colors and moving objects are more likely to attract a baby's attention. Some mobiles readily available combine interesting shapes, bright colors, and ingenious movement. Infants seem to gain added enjoyment from things they can move, and these teach them that they have some control over their environment. Toys of different sizes, shapes, textures, and colors add to the learning experience. Parents should provide a combination of soft and furry playthings, like little toy animals, with objects that are smooth and well-defined, like light blocks or geometrical shapes. Of course, these objects should not be sharp or heavy, which could constitute a danger to your child. At first these are just interesting toys for children to taste and feel, but what these toys really do is give them an introduction to other creatures that inhabit the world and the basic geometric shapes that all things are made of.

Once your child ventures out of the crib, he or she is exposed to a whole new world. Parents play a big part in this adventure, because they control their children's movement and the objects with which they come in contact. Whenever you are with your children, indoors or out, shopping or visiting, try to expose them to as much visual and physical stimuli as possible. There is no danger of overloading them because you are not really asking them to do anything difficult; you are simply familiarizing them with a broad range of objects and experiences. When you accompany your children on these excursions, and so help them to learn, they can regard you as partners in learning from the earliest stages.

The most important thing parents can do when they are with their children is to talk to them. We often chuckle when we hear adults talking to babies in a contrived voice, even before they are old enough to understand the words being said. In fact, the child is being told the names and functions of many different things. It really doesn't matter what the child understands at this stage. The important point is that the child is hearing the same words over and over again, and begins to associate them with different objects and behaviors. As your child watches you with that intent, friendly little smile, underneath it all there is an intelligence at work and the first stages of speech are underway. That is why it is wise to pronounce words properly. You really cannot talk to your child too much. Not only does it signify your love and concern, you are laying a foundation for growth later on.

Speaking is also important because it is a precursor to reading. The words children recognize and associate with different objects are the same they will be reading. I am a firm believer in introducing children to reading at the earliest possible age. Although it may be quite a while before children start to read, it is a wonderful practice to start reading to them while they are still in the crib. It is another way for the child to become familiar with words, and the child will observe you as you read aloud. There are so many wonderful children's books and in so many different forms: cloth, cardboard, and paper, with a variety of interesting and innovative illustrations. The small cloth or fabric books with more illustrations than words are practically indestructible, and are particularly well-suited to infants. The idea is to introduce children to the world of books at the earliest possible age so they will view them as objects of enjoyment rather than drudgery. The reason this is so important is that a child who does not love books will face an uphill struggle through his entire educational experience.

Nursery School and Kindergarten Years

In the early years before your child enters the first grade in elementary school, you need to spend the maximum amount of time with your youngster. The work of child development specialists has confirmed over and over again that it is crucial to build a strong foundation during these early years to encourage growth. Throughout this time you will follow the familiar advice of speaking and reading frequently to your child. You will also encourage the preliminary skills needed for writing and problem solving.

In today's world of busy schedules and working parents, we all wonder how to find enough time to spend with our children. One way is to include our young children in our daily activities, whether around the house or outside errands.

You should talk continuously to your child. If you are washing clothes tell your child how the washing machine works and describe the purpose of detergent. If you are cooking a meal, show your child what uncooked food looks like, describe how different foods are mixed together to create certain dishes, and explain the process of cooking, warning them of course about things they should not do themselves. If you are building an outdoor gym set, let your child watch how you do it and explain different mechanical principles involved. When you shop, mention the names of different foods as you walk up and down the aisle and explain where they come from. In all of these activities, try to find a way for your child to be a participant rather than an observer. It might be something as simple as getting food from the shelf, helping to load clothes into the washer, or fetching a tool. Learning is much more exciting when one is a participant. You should involve your child in these activities very early, usually at two or three years of age.

I want you to think very carefully for a moment about what I am recommending. Daily responsibilities like those I have described are something you have to fulfill anyway, and they are often a real chore, so why not turn them into learning experiences that benefit both you and your child. The act of teaching will distract you, and your child will learn about the world while spending some quality time with you. Besides, the close association will continue the process of bonding that began shortly after birth.

In addition to contact from everyday activities, you should set aside a special time—each day if possible—to spend with your child. During this time you should read to your child, discuss what you have read, and answer questions. Your child will look forward to these sessions, and you will find that they help to foster a closer relationship. Even though competing activities invariably come up, you should find a way to prevent them from interfering with your special time.

It is never too soon to introduce your child to the world of books. Even a child of two or three can benefit from a trip to the library. Given the large amount of reading materials available for young children, most libraries have extensive collections organized by reading level and subject. Taking your child to the library and letting him or her browse will be a memorable experience. Permit your youngsters to pick out a few books that catch their interest, and read to them whenever you have time. Even though your toddler cannot yet read, point out the words as you pronounce them, and add your own explanations and editorial comments to make the material more understandable. Be sure to include some of the children's classics in your selection; they seem to please every generation. If you discover some books that your child particularly likes, try to purchase them from your local bookstore. Small children seem never to tire of hearing the same story over and over again. Keeping favorite books helps to cultivate an appreciation for them.

As soon as children are able to hold a pencil or crayon, often before their second birthday, you should give them something to write on. It doesn't have to be canvas—even old scrap paper or a discarded paper bag used to bring in the groceries will do. Even though the first efforts may be barely more than an unrecognizable scribble, you have just introduced your child to the world of writing. You should participate actively in this exercise, showing your child how to hold the writing instrument, and tracing out a few shapes that might remind her of something that is part of her world. With time and practice, you can begin to show her how to draw more elaborate shapes, or copy letters in the alphabet. Be sure to pronounce the letters, and write some of the words she has seen in books.

It is best to encourage children to scribble or write almost every day if possible. If you see their interest starts to wane, you can add additional colors to the crayon box, or switch to other mediums such as water and finger paints. Some children will take to these activities more readily than others, but with patience and persistence you can help accustom your child to something that will be a recurring part of his or her future educational experience.

Another skill your child will be required to master is problem solving. You can help children develop this skill at a very early age and have fun doing it. You begin with the simple process of counting fingers or other objects before a child is two years old, and then progress with the introduction of basic arithmetic operations such as addition and subtraction. You will have more success if you turn the exercise into a game and quiz your child about the answers. The object is to start developing the powers of reasoning and logic at a very early age. This can also be done with an explanation of how to tell time, which requires the manipulation of numbers. Try to get your child to write down numerical values as you talk about them. Educational toys, like toy clocks that help children tell time or puzzles that challenge the mind, are also an excellent way to develop problem-solving skills.

Toys that require children to build structures with different geometrical shapes are also good for developing problem-solving skills. You don't have to spend a lot of money to challenge your child; even a simple maze on a piece of paper will do the trick. Once again, the main thing is that parents need to be partners in learning with their children.

Parents can't be with their children every minute of the day, of course, and there are times when youngsters want peace and quiet themselves. On such occasions you should make sure that your child has something constructive to work on. Too many parents put their children in front of a television set just to get them out of the way. A child should probably watch some television just to see different scenery and people, and hear various sounds and words. Some educational television shows provide an opportunity to see places and things that we would not otherwise encounter. And sometimes youngsters want to watch a program or cartoon just for the fun of it, and that's fine too. The important point is that no child should be sitting in front of a television set for an extended period of time. Just remember that television is a passive experience in which everything is boiled down to appeal to the broadest possible audience. The real purpose of most television programs is to make money by advertising commercial products to consumers, and entertainment is only a means to that end. So, rather than sending your child off to watch TV, it will be far more beneficial if you can get him to read—or even look—at books instead.

Since most people work these days, including mothers with small children, there will be substantial blocks of time that parents cannot spend with their youngsters. In such cases it is important that children receive quality day care or attend a good nursery school or kindergarten. The objective is to find an organization that will provide the same kinds of activities that you would offer, with the same close attention, and not merely babysit until you pick up the child later on. The cost for these services can be quite high, but the investment is well worth it. Even if you are not working, you should consider enrolling your child in preschool. Programs such as Head Start have shown that students will be more successful later on if they are taught basic skills at a very early age. A good preschool offers the opportunity for your child to receive education from a trained instructor and develop valuable social skills from interacting with other youngsters. This experience leads to a smoother transition when your child begins elementary school.

Elementary School

Once children enroll in elementary school, there are activities that parents can offer at home to enhance their learning skills. At this point, I will not discuss those activities related to their formal classroom instruction; that discussion will come in part 3. In addition, I will not provide specific methods designed to help master the three R's: reading, writing, and arithmetic; that discussion will appear in part 2. The emphasis here is on activities at home that will help children prepare to master these more formal skills.

Even though children will assume more independence when they enter elementary school, it remains important to include them in your daily activities. You should continue to talk to your child but, by the age of five or six, your discussion and your child's involvement should be at a higher, more challenging level. For example, the next time you take your six-year-old to the food store, ask him or her to read the road signs and explain to you what they mean. Then ask your child to read the labels as you walk up and own the aisles. You may also want to ask your child to explain where the food comes from. If you have some extra time, you could examine a few labels, describing the concepts of ingredients, nutritional content, weight, and price. When you return home, your child might help you prepare portions of the meal. Many other daily activities, like those I described earlier, can also be approached on a higher level. If you do this properly, the whole exercise will appear to be more of a game than work, providing some stimulation and fun for both of you.

Parents can converse about the things their children like or dislike, relationships with friends and enemies, and maybe even some of the issues that have preoccupied philosophers over the centuries, like love, religion, life, and death. In the process, give children plenty of time to talk, which will help to develop their powers of expression. Extend the discussion a few steps beyond their present understanding to stimulate their curiosity. Listen carefully to their concerns and try to correct faulty reasoning. Answer children's questions in an understandable and earnest manner. Children will gain a general education, from their parent's perspective, and this will further reinforce the parent's role as a partner in learning.

One of the best ways to spend special time with children is to take them to a museum or art gallery. These are fascinating places for children as young as five or six. I realize that the accessibility of such places depends on where you live, but you should try to visit them even if they are far away. Because I reside in the Washington, D.C., area, I have ready access to the Smithsonian Institution and the National Gallery of Art. At the National Museum of Natural History, I can show my children that the world is inhabited by far more species than those they have seen in the neighborhood. At the National Museum of American History, my youngsters learn that our country has a rich and varied political, social, technological, and cultural history. At the National Air and Space Museum, my children discover that man has flown in more interesting and sophisticated vehicles than the commercial airplanes they have traveled in. And at the National Gallery of Art, we can learn about the wonderful masterpieces created through the ages by the best artists in the world. Such experiences engender wonder and the love of knowledge in a child, and your presence helps to enhance that feeling. Be sure to talk about the various things you see, in words that children can understand—reading wall cards to them can sometimes be a good way to explain exhibits.

If you have been reading to your children from an early age, they should appreciate the wonderful stories and knowledge contained in books. Your efforts and the instruction they receive in school will enable them to read at an early age. You should continue to take your children to the library and let them pick out the books that interest them. While we all know that some books are better than others, practically any book is beneficial because it develops a child's ability to read, to understand sentence structure, and to reason. A good approach to enhance reading education is for you to read for a while, and then allow your child to do the same. Help children pronounce words with which they have difficulty, and explain the meaning of any words they do not understand. After you have both finished reading, you can quiz your children on what the story was all about and how it might relate to their own lives. Direct participation by the parent takes the frustration out of reading, and makes the experience more enjoyable for the child. With practice, parents should gradually be able to withdraw so their children can read alone. Then they can ask for your assistance only when they need it.

If children have been writing from an early age, a pencil should feel very natural in their hand. Many children can make recognizable markings before their third birthday. Encourage them to practice writing the letters of the alphabet, and offer assistance where needed. After children have learned how to print and then write, show them the value of these skills by encouraging them to write their own stories. Edit children's work by correcting any grammatical or spelling errors. Teach them new words that are more descriptive and appropriate than the ones they have used. Make suggestions about other things that might happen in the story, and encourage children to develop changes on their own. Then help children polish the story into a finished work. Show the story to other members of the family or their friends. Your participation and encouragement will help your children feel at ease with writing, and encourage them to produce an even better story the next time. Save these stories in a looseleaf binder so you can see your children's progression over time.

Parents should also have their children draw—with the caveat that most youngsters will not become professional artists, and the experience will prove frustrating to some. But the act of drawing can teach children to be observant about the world in which they live and helps develop manual dexterity. Encourage children to draw different things inside and outside the house. If you have artistic skills yourself, show them that just about all objects are composed of various combinations of the basic geometric shapes. With practice, just about anyone can improve her drawing ability, even though there are limits on how far some can progress.

Developing problem-solving skills is another area where you can help children during the elementary-school years. Students are taught basic arithmetic in the first grade, at five or six years of age. If you have already taught them basic skills in addition and subtraction, work next on multiplication and then division. While some of these skills, like learning the multiplication tables, consist of brute memorization, you should help your child to understand the concepts involved. Work with him on the basic geometric shapes and teach him the concepts of area and volume. You can introduce a child to fractions by simple things you do around the house, like cutting a pie into quarters and then subdividing it further. With your child by your side, explain carefully what you are doing, and then answer questions. Also look for occasions where you can challenge children, such as asking them to figure out how much change you are due at the grocery store, or mapping the best route on the family vacation. By developing children's problem-solving skills at an early age, you can improve their ability and comfort level to deal with such challenges at school.

The advice about abstaining from too much television still applies, now more than ever. Children in elementary school have a tendency to become addicted to the TV set, often spending several hours a day as passive observers. An even greater danger is video games, which allow the child to be an active participant, but in an activity that gobbles up big chunks of time. While it can be argued that video games can teach some of the basic computer-use skills, most of them do not go very far in this direction. I realize that just about every child wants to play these games because they are fun, but parents need to limit the amount of time spent on them each day. Your child will be better off becoming involved in sports and playing a musical instrument. At least these activities develop useful skills that can be developed and refined further, and may even serve as a discipline that carries over to the classroom. Being athletically or musically gifted can even lead to college scholarships. How can you ever get such a good return from an investment in video games?

Junior High School

Children usually enter junior high (or middle) school at about twelve years of age. If you have been doing a good job with your child in the early years, then many of the things I am going to say now will already occur naturally. The objective is to create the right environment at home, and keep children on the right track so they can continue to progress. I will discuss the familiar subjects of how you can set the stage at home for better reading, writing, and problem solving, but I will add a few other important suggestions for junior-high-school students.

Not only should you include these youngsters in your daily activities, they should now be old enough to participate in activities on their own. I am a firm believer in assigning selected household chores to children, because they build responsibility and discipline. The chores may be as simple as cleaning a room, setting the dinner table, or mowing the grass on a regular basis. Through these activities, children learn that they have to budget their time. They also learn that it takes initiative to start these projects and perseverance to complete them. These skills transfer readily to the classroom for starting assignments and completing them. Please note that I do not recommend that you burden children with too many household duties, because this would take time from their studies. School must always be the principal occupation of children at this age. You will also find that children respond more readily to chores when they receive an allowance for them. This has the added benefit of connecting reward with effort, which also carries over to the classroom.

An interest in learning can also be generated from field trips and family outings. Many elementary and junior high schools make field trips a part of their curriculum. Earlier I mentioned trips to the museum as a way to create wonder and the love of knowledge in a child. Older children will benefit even more than younger children from visiting museums because they know more about the world and can relate much of what they see to what they have learned in school. Moreover, trips to museums generate even more interest in school studies, because now they can relate to what they learn in a more tangible way.

Another way to connect school knowledge with family entertainment is to make a little extra effort on a family vacation. If you plan to visit a place that has some historical significance, find out where the key sites are located and learn what happened there. By being able to relate this information to children, and explain how it applies to their present-day life, you may be able to turn what is often viewed as a humdrum experience into an exciting event. In fact, *you* may end up learning more than you bargained for if your child supplies some additional information learned in school. Remember, you are your child's partner in learning.

If you have been following the advice I gave earlier, you child should love books by the time he or she reaches junior high school. Children undoubtedly will read a number of books for their classroom assignments, but you should encourage them to read during leisure hours as well. There are so many occasions when children can turn to books. Take a rainy day when a youngster sits around the house complaining about nothing to do, or while waiting in the doctor's or dentist's office for an appointment, or taking a long trip in the car on a family vacation. (I'm sure that you can think of many other appropriate times as well.) When children complain about not having anything good to read, take them to the library or bookstore and let them pick out what they want. You should also encourage your child to read some good literature. If you are having difficulty making selections of appropriate books, ask your youngster's English teacher for advice. The main objective is to keep children reading as much as possible, because in the process they will build up their vocabulary, improve their understanding of sentence structure, and learn more about the world.

During the junior-high-school years, from about twelve to fourteen years of age, you should continue to encourage children to write their own stories. As a fellow author once told me, when we write we learn so much about ourselves and at the same time develop our craft. A short story or a poem will suffice. Encourage children to write about something they feel is significant, or are particularly interested in. As before, sit down with your youngster and correct spelling, grammatical, or logical errors. At this stage do not be afraid to tell her where her work is weak or how she might have presented it differently. But be sure to use words of encouragement to build up her confidence, rather than words of criticism that will lead to frustration and despair. If she has produced something that is noteworthy, not only show it to friends and family, but also enter it in a contest for budding young authors. If your child really gets into the habit of writing, build a portfolio that he can use to illustrate his work in the same manner as an artist. Believe me, it makes a wonderful impression on a junior-high-school English teacher. The very least that your child will get from these efforts is better command of the English language, and more polished prose in the classroom.

Problem-solving skills are vital because they are just about the most important asset a person can have in the workplace. If you have been following my advice, you should have noticed not only an improvement in your children's ability to solve problems, but also a willingness to tackle them. Here are some additional ideas you can use to develop problem-solving skills outside of the classroom for junior-high students. If you are engaged in a home project in which you have to figure out how much lumber, concrete, or fertilizer to buy, let your children use their knowledge of mathematics to figure the supplies you need to purchase. When income tax time rolls around, give your youngsters an idea of what you have to go through, without burdening her with unnecessary details or headaches. If you are grappling with a particularly knotty problem at work, explain it to your children in simple terms and seek their advice. By acquainting young people with the type of problems you have to tackle at home and on the job, you will give them a better idea of the adult skills they will need. And this will help them to understand why they need to work hard at school to develop these skills.

An additional piece of advice is especially relevant to junior-high school students. Children of this age have impressionable minds and are susceptible to all different kinds of influences. If your youngster hangs around other children who spend their time watching television and playing video games, then you should not expect much different from him. In some cases, children may be influenced by very bad associates and end up in trouble with the law. Try to get your child to mix with others who have a love of knowledge and books, and you will see the same values reflected when your son or daughter is with you. The junior-high-school years are a turning point in many people's lives. How well children do in school can determine what kind of academic track they enter and the youngsters with whom they will associate during their school years. It is important to get children on the right track early.

Adapting to Your Child's Needs

It never ceases to amaze me how two or more children of the same parents can be so different. The same formula for birth produces different appearances, different personalities, and—most significant here—different aptitudes. No two children learn in exactly the same way. Some learn better through their sense of hearing, while others learn physically by doing, and still others learn best by intellectualizing in an abstract way. I happen to have three children who absorb knowledge in each of these different modes, and I will relate some of my experiences to help you adapt best to your own youngster's needs.

My oldest daughter Heidi is adept at using her sense of hearing to learn. Even before her third birthday, she was an avid listener. These skills carry over today, whether the discussion involves interpersonal communication, media presentations, or formal lectures in the classroom. She has a rare and uncanny ability to concentrate totally on what is being said, and to remember intricate details from the discussion. Heidi is a very well-rounded person who also uses her mental and physical capabilities to learn, but it became clear to my wife and me that her special skills for listening would enable her to excel. We worked hard to develop her other skills, while using her keen ability to listen to keep her abreast of material presented in school. For example, we asked Heidi's teachers to allow her to sit in the front row of the classroom, so that she could hear everything the teacher had to say. Heidi continues to sit in the front row of all of her classes. We have noticed that Heidi has become more interested in her studies with the passage of time. She used my study methods presented in my earlier book, *Getting Straight A's*, and was able to make straight A's in her first semester at college. Heidi is proof that getting children on the right track, and playing to their strengths rather than their weaknesses, pays big dividends later on.

My middle child, Dana, learns best in a physical way. We noticed that Dana liked to scribble before her second birthday. She has used more pencils, crayons, and paper than my other two children combined. As Dana grew older, her use of these skills and mastery of them has become more pronounced. I do not have to encourage her in this direction, because as soon as she gets home from school she takes a big stack of the typing paper from my desk and starts drawing everything in sight. She creates her own world by sketching things around the house, from the newspaper, or from her imagination. When I succeed in getting her to read a book, she eventually puts it down and then starts writing her own stories. Then she illustrates them and draws a suitable cover to make her own book. My wife and I try to play to this strength by encouraging Dana to make notes in class or write summaries of the books she is studying. As long as we can keep a pencil in her hand and a piece of paper in front of her, she is willing to pursue an activity for a much longer period of time. She really enjoys the act of writing, and sometimes talks about becoming an author herself. As long as we can keep her writing, we will have a much better chance of making these dreams come true, and helping her to succeed in school in the meantime.

My youngest child, Chris, relies heavily on his intellectual abilities to learn. There are times when he participates in other activities with his siblings, but his forte is clearly the intellectual mode. This characteristic became apparent before his second birthday when he insisted that my wife or I read him a story. He has a voracious appetite for books and never seems to tire of reading them. Chris learned to read at a very early age, and I often find him reading to himself in some nook or cranny in the house. Sometimes I see him in my study, browsing through the multitude of books I have on my shelf. Chris has amassed quite a collection of titles for his own library. One of his favorites is the *Guinness Book of Records*, which he reads for long periods of time with a look of fascination on his face. My wife and I try to keep his reading appetite nourished by supplying him with a steady supply of books from the library, bookstore, or book club. You can tell when children really love the written word, by the way they ask you to explain to them *exactly* what a word means in a given context. They are also enthusiastic about telling you what they have read. The love of books is a clear indication that a child prefers the intellectual approach, as evidenced by my son Chris.

As you attempt to adapt to your own child's needs, one consideration is of paramount importance. You will not be able to sit back and merely advise your child on the proper course of action. All parents should be role models for their children. Practice the behavior that you want your children to observe. I try to do this myself by the things I do around the house. When I tell my children that books are fun to read, they know I am serious because they see me reading regularly. My children know how I feel about writing, because they often see me sitting at my word processor working on books like this one. And when I tell them they will need to know mathematics later on in life, this is reinforced when they see me working at home on statistical problems from my job. The proper mode of behavior is summarized precisely by the advice from the National Commission on Excellence in Education:

PRINCIPLE 2
You must be a living example of what you expect your children to honor and to emulate.

SUMMARY

Part 1
The Importance of Your Child's Education

PRINCIPLE 1
You bear a responsibility to participate actively in your child's education.

PRINCIPLE 2
You must be a living example of what you expect your children to honor and to emulate.

MASTERING THE THREE R'S

Overview of the Basic Skills

The three R's—reading, writing, and arithmetic—must be mastered because they are basic requirements for functioning well in the modern-day world. As your children go through school and into the working world, they will be required to use these skills over and over again. A child who truly understands the three R's will have a solid foundation that will support all subsequent learning. A child who has not mastered the three R's will experience repeated frustration, and will miss much of the material presented in the classroom.

Everything starts with reading, because it is the basic mechanism by which we gather information about the world. Many children learn the mechanics of reading before they enter kindergarten, and improve steadily as they progress through school. They can read from a complicated book, accurately pronouncing the words and using the proper inflections. And yet, if you give them a test on what they have read, their scores indicate that they have not understood very much of the content. The problem is that most students were never taught the proper way to read a book. They merely pick up the book and start reading, not knowing how to organize the material into a framework, not asking critical questions about the material presented, and not being able to relate the material to their own lives. In this section, I will show you how to help children read a book properly, so they can get the most out of it.

Writing is a critical skill because it is the principal mechanism by which we express our thoughts to others. We may be capable of brilliant thoughts, but others will not be able to appreciate them if we are unable to express ourselves clearly. I have seen over and over again that many students do poorly on exams because they are unable to describe their understanding of a subject accurately and comprehensively. One problem for many people is that their writing is a flow of consciousness, just like the words that come out of our mouths when we speak. While it is good to have a conversational tone, all writers know that they must present their material in a logical and coherent way to be effective. In what follows, I will show you how to teach children the fundamentals of good writing, so they can score high on examinations and written assignments, and enjoy the act of writing in the process.

Arithmetic, or more broadly, mathematics, has become a basic requirement of life because we use it in so much of what we do. Everyone has to pay bills and taxes, and more and more people are using mathematics at work. If your child wants to enter a scientific or technical field, he or she will have to have an understanding of higher mathematics. Many students shy away from technical subjects in school because they are afraid of the mathematics. Their problem stems largely from not mastering the material at an early stage when it was simple. As studies get more complex, mathematics becomes the most dreaded of all disciplines for the unprepared. Students complain that they can't understand what is going on because everything seems to be in a foreign language. In this section, I will show you how to develop a solid foundation in mathematics for your children so they will not experience these problems later on. It all comes from knowing the proper progression of topics and mastering the fundamentals at each stage. With the proper attitude and some hard work, your child may join the select few who say that mathematics is their favorite subject.

1

Reading

Thomas Carlyle, the Scottish historian, once remarked that, "All that mankind has done, thought, gained or been: it is lying as in magic preservation in the pages of books."

Just think about Carlyle's statement for a moment. The entire history of the world, and how we progressed to our present state of knowledge, can be found in books written through the ages. Through books, your child will have an opportunity to meet the greatest thinkers, even though they lived in a different time or place. When we read their works, it is as if they are sitting right beside us, and we are their only audience. Books contain the purest expression of their thoughts, worked and reworked into perfection. When we read books, we are transported to another world, one of knowledge, insight, enjoyment, and feeling. How much of these qualities we obtain from books depends upon our skill in reading them. To get the most from books, we must expend as much effort in reading them as authors exert in writing them.

More to the point, children are required to read a number of books and articles as they progress through school. Younger children typically are expected to do a certain amount of reading in class, in part to help develop their reading skills. As they get older, children are asked to read books as homework assignments or to prepare for upcoming subjects in the classroom. Eventually youngsters reach a point where they must read a number of books for a research paper or to learn about material that extends what was presented in class. How well children do in these assignments depends on how well they understand the material presented.

Teaching Your Child How to Read

There is extensive literature on how parents and educators can teach small children to read. Some of the methods can be used with children before their third birthday. (I have listed some of these works in the references at the back of this book.) Some educators believe that the best way to teach children how to read is through "phonics," while others are convinced that the "look and say" method works best. With phonics you teach children how to read by telling them about the sounds of letters—or combinations of letters—and then showing them how to blend these letters together to read the entire word. With the look-and-say approach, you show children a picture or representation of an object with the word printed underneath, and encourage them to memorize the group of letters that make up the word. Of my three children, two learned to read by using phonics, while one learned by using the look-and-say method. I did not see any significant difference in reading proficiency or speed of accomplishment between the two approaches, and therefore, I am going to stay out of the debate. What I will do instead is offer a few simple pointers that you can use, regardless of the approach to learning to read.

As I noted earlier, the most important thing you can do is to read often to a small child. You cannot begin this too early, even while the child is still in the crib. Start off by reading books with very simple one-syllable words that have a concrete reference to something. This will enable you to point to the object being referred to, whether it is something like a piece of furniture, a pet, a part of the anatomy, etc. Children's books with pictures associated with the words are especially instructive. As you point to an object or word, pronounce it very slowly and clearly. On subsequent readings, go over the words in the same way, and occasionally quiz your child to say the word or object you point to. Sometimes sitting down with a magazine and repeating the names of objects helps to drive home the association. Repetition is the means by which children learn that a given class of things bears the same name, whenever it is referred to.

To help youngsters distinguish between different objects in a given class of things, you will need to teach them some adjectives. You should begin this as soon as your child is able to speak. Knowing that something is big or small, or long or short, helps a child appreciate the great diversity in the world. Being able to distinguish between the basic color groups is also something that should come very early in the instruction process. You will find that most books for young readers mix and match these basic distinctions in a creative way that will enable your offspring to grasp the concept and be entertained at the same time. You should be right there with your child, helping him or her to learn these identifying characteristics, and then extending them to other things in your surroundings as a way of establishing the concept. As you advance to more complicated material, you will be challenged in your efforts to teach your child that some words refer to different states of being or feeling, such as *strong* and *weak*, or *happy* and *sad*. Sometimes these concepts can be taught with a simple concrete representation, such as a person trying to lift a heavy object, or the expression that appears on a happy face as opposed to a sad one.

You will also be challenged in your efforts to help your child recognize and say more complicated words that have multiple syllables and unusual pronunciations. Parents should begin teaching children more difficult words as soon as they have mastered simple ones. A basic part of teaching children how to read is showing them how to break up a word into syllables, pronounce each part, and string them together to say or read a word. This is easier if your child knows how to say and write the alphabet. Knowing the alphabet will help her recognize the letters and words she sees in the books you are reading to her. It is important for children to become familiar with both upper-case and lower-case letters, so they do not become confused in the process. At an appropriate point, you should teach your child the distinction between vowels (a,e,i,o,u) and consonants (all other letters). It also helps to teach your youngster the little rhymes we learned as children about appropriate usage, such as "*i* before *e* except after *c*." You should teach your child how to recognize and say frequently recurring consonant combinations such as *th* and *ng*, as well as common consonant-vowel combinations such as *gu*. Learning common prefixes and suffixes will also help your son or daughter to see that many of the words in the English language have common derivatives. The really difficult part will be teaching your child that sometimes combinations of letters are pronounced differently, and other times words are not pronounced the way they appear.

I do not plan to say much more about the basic mechanics of reading. As noted, consult some of the books listed in the references if you wish to learn about the various approaches that have been used for teaching very young children how to read. Your child will receive formal instruction on reading skills once he or she enters school, since much of the early curriculum deals with this subject. What I am most interested in doing here is to show you how to help your child *understand* and *retain* the material presented in books. As you will see, reading and understanding are two different things.

Helping Children to Understand What They Have Read

Over the past several decades, many researchers have explored different approaches for teaching people to comprehend and retain what they have read. Some of the early work in this field goes back to 1946, when Francis Robinson wrote a landmark book titled, *Effective Study*. In this work he proposed a reading method called the SQ3R, which stands for *S*urvey, *Q*uestion, *R*ead, *R*eview, and *R*ecite. This basically describes the order of things readers should do to understand what they are reading. In 1954, Thomas Staton wrote *How to Study*, which proposed a slightly different approach for mastering written material. Staton labeled his approach the PQRST, and recommended that readers *P*review, *Q*uestion, *R*ead, *S*tate, and *T*est, in that order. A few decades later in 1972, Mortimer Adler and Charles Van Doren wrote *How to Read a Book*, which synthesized and extended much of the earlier material on how to read effectively.

These various reading systems propose different methods for reviewing summary information in books, such as topic sentences, boldface type, and summary paragraphs, before the reader actually starts reading. In general, where these methods differ is on the proper order for conducting these reviews. There is no consensus on which of these reading systems is best, so I am not going to review them here. Instead, I will present the method I have found most useful over the years for reading books.

First, impress your child that reading is a leisure activity. As such, suggest that your youngster wear comfortable clothing and find a suitable place to sit. We all have our favorite spots for reading. Mine actually differ, depending on what I am reading. I like a big easy chair if I am reading a novel, and prefer a desk if I also have to write while reading. Some people, like my oldest daughter, prefer to work in bed, whether reading or writing. Beware: If you become too comfortable your reading will be less efficient, and you may even fall asleep. Research has shown that slight muscular tension increases both efficiency and mental acuity. You should experiment to help your children find the reading location(s) that works best for them. If you select places that they associate with reading or studying, they may find it easier to get into a groove as soon as they sit down.

A key consideration in helping your child select a place to read is to choose a spot that is relatively quiet and out of the way of major household traffic. Small children are easily distracted, so you do not want to put them too close to irresistible temptations such as food, television, video games, or other children. People, both young and mature alike, have different capacities for coping with noise. Some can work efficiently in the noisiest places while others are easily distracted. Ask your child about the suitability of the spot you have both selected, and make an adjustment if necessary. If your child still complains about noise, play some gentle background music on the stereo or radio, which will help her to relax and screen out other distracting sounds.

Always choose a place with ample light. For some unfathomable reason, children seem to gravitate to a dark corner. Inadequate light may tire or otherwise harm children's eyes. Research has shown that our eyes are much less likely to become tired under indirect light from a fluorescent lamp than under direct light. Whatever source of light you use, make sure that it shines evenly on the page from overhead or behind the reader.

Now that we have finished with preliminaries, let's assume that you and your child are about to begin reading. The book might be on science or social studies, or some other subject your child is studying. How should your child go about reading that book?

It is important to show youngsters the proper way to approach a book rather than allowing them to lunge into the first chapter. You should do this before your child enters school. First mention the cover and title page, so that they get an overall impression of what the book is all about. Point out that subtitles and other information on the cover usually provide insights about the contents of the book. Next, look up the name and location of the publisher, and explain that firm's role. Make sure you read the short statement about the author's background and experiences, usually at the back of the book, to give your child some perspective on the author. Following this, read the preface or introduction to find out why the author wrote the book, and how he or she plans to present the material. Finally read the table of contents to learn about the overall structure and specific content of the book.

By this time your child should have a good idea of what the book is all about. You can teach your child to be a more alert and careful observer by playing a little game. Close the book and put it out of sight. Ask your child to repeat the title of the book, and tell you the name of the person who wrote it and something about the author. If your child seems to be struggling, be patient and give him a hint. Remember, the object is to enjoy the game.

Next ask your child to tell you something about the content of the book. Here again, supply hints to see if you can refresh your youngster's memory. Your child will be more alert the next time he picks up a book, just in case you might quiz him again.

Your child is still not ready to begin reading. Skim through the first chapter to gain an overview, in other words, "look at the forest before inspecting the trees." Point out to your child that different sections of the chapter have a very different look. Some of the print is very large and bold compared to the other parts. And sometimes there are boxes with summary information, or pictures and graphs that illustrate a concept being presented. Explain to your child that this format is designed to make it easier to read the book and remember its content. Children who learn these details early will have a much easier time reading books in school.

As you scan the first chapter, ask your child to read introductory and summary paragraphs, major and minor headings, conclusions and summaries. If your youngster has difficulty, provide help with the pronunciation of words, and explain what they mean. Look at the pictures and illustrations, and ask your child to tell you what they represent. You are not wasting time, because this approach helps children develop a framework for organizing the material when they actually start to read it. This exercise will improve their comprehension and retention. Although you may not realize it, you have just transmitted a lot of information to your child's subconscious mind. You should encourage your child to preview each chapter of the book in the same fashion.

In general, children should use the same methods of previewing for other books they will use in their studies, whether the works are about history, social science, mathematics, government, or any other technical field.

One exception is that you should not encourage your
child to preview literature in the same way. With a novel
or mystery, the object is to develop the story, or build and
preserve the suspense for as long as possible. If children
jump ahead by reading the middle or back of the book
they will spoil the plot, just as viewing the middle or end
of a movie before the beginning ruins it for us.

Reading Actively, Not Passively

You are almost ready to start reading the first chapter
with your child. Before you commence, you should make
sure that your child knows how to read. We see so many
children who can read very glibly from a book, with all
of the right pronunciations, and yet they are hard pressed
to tell us its meaning when they finish. The problem is
that many children know how to read words, but don't
know how to string them all together to grasp a concept.
The key to successful comprehension is that the youngster must read in an active rather than passive manner.
Active readers not only comprehend more than passive
readers, they find the experience of reading to be more
interesting and enjoyable. A child who reads a book without understanding its message will be more bored than a
child sitting in a corner doing nothing at all. Do you
know whether your child is an active or passive reader?
Let's find out.

  If your child is a passive reader, he or she simply goes
through the motions of reading words without concentrating on what is being read. There is no attempt to
understand the author's message, or the relationship
between ideas presented. The child is unable to relate the
material to his or her own experiences. You can tell when
youngsters are reading passively because their attention

begins to drift and they start to talk about other things they would rather be doing, such as playing with their toys or friends. We should not be surprised that these youngsters find reading to be boring. They are wasting their time, because passive reading does not impart any knowledge about the subject.

How is the active reader different from the passive reader? If your child is an active reader, he or she will read a book in a very deliberate manner, sorting out all of the information presented and understanding the relationships between various ideas and concepts. You should explain to your child that understanding a concept is not the same as rote memorization, since it is possible for someone to memorize a long passage without understanding anything about it. If children really understand what they have read, they should be able to explain it in their own words and still preserve the author's intended meaning. That is why it is so important for you, the parent, to ask children to describe what they have read after they have put the book away. If they falter, you need to go over the material again and explain to your child what the author meant and how the various ideas tie together.

Obviously we cannot spend all of our lives reading books with our children. The goal is to get youngsters to a point where they can read with understanding on their own, shortly after they enter school. To reach this level, your sons and daughters must ask questions while they read. Give them some examples, such as: What is this book all about? What does it say in detail—in other words, what are the specific things said in the book? How does the material I have read supplement what I am learning in class? Active readers try to relate what they have read to their own knowledge and experiences. Your children should explore whether the information has changed their knowledge, behavior, or view of the world.

Your youngster will become a more astute, active reader if he or she also reads critically. Reading critically means constantly questioning what the author is saying. Some critical questions that your child might ask: What issues is the author trying to address and how does he or she do so? What are the assumptions the author has made in the book and what is the basis for making them? (Explain to your child what an assumption is.) Are the author's statements based on facts, experiences, knowledge, or opinions? (Explain each of these concepts to your child.) Are the author's statements objective or do they reflect a definite bias? (Give your child examples of each.) Do you agree or disagree with what the author is saying, and what is the basis for your assessment? If you disagree with the author, is it because he or she has not offered enough evidence for the assertions, or is the reasoning flawed? (Here again, examples are helpful.) These questions probably do not occur to most children—or even adults, for that matter! Although your youngster may not know the answers, by attempting to answer these questions your child will go a long way toward becoming an active reader.

It is important children know that the questioning process does not end after they have finished reading a chapter. Tell them to reflect on what they have read and quiz themselves to see if they have mastered the material before moving on to the next chapter. If youngsters properly assess what they have learned, they should be able to describe their new knowledge in their own words. This exercise does wonders for improving comprehension, because children know that they will have to test their understanding before they continue with their reading.

In addition to the questioning process, your child should seek comprehension and mastery of every significant point in the book.

In order to gain a full understanding of the author's message, your child must be able to read and understand all of the words he or she uses. To succeed, children must learn to use the dictionary to look up the meaning of every word they encounter but do not understand. Although a child can sometimes understand the meaning of a word by the way it is used in the context of a sentence, this is not the best way to master that word. The dictionary contains the exact meaning(s) of words and lots of other pertinent information. It is very important that you teach your children how to use a dictionary. Point out the origin of words, their spelling and pronunciation, the parts of speech, single and multiple meanings, and so forth. When children begin to study science in school, it is especially important for them to understand the meaning of scientific and technical terms; if they cannot understand the terms, they will not be able to understand the scientific principle being discussed.

Looking up words in the dictionary will not only help children gain a full understanding of the author's message, it will expand and develop their vocabulary as well. Children with a better command over words will be able to express themselves more clearly in both speaking and writing. This will give them an advantage when making oral presentations in class or writing answers to examination questions, not just in English but in all of their classes.

As a parent of three children, I know firsthand just how difficult it is to get youngsters to use the dictionary. I encourage my children to have a dictionary at their side whenever they sit down to read. However, getting them to use it is another matter. I have to tell them repeatedly to look up words they do not know, rather than ask me, but the dictionary usually remains dormant unless I am nearby. Since a dictionary can be inherently boring, you can make the task a little easier by providing them with a children's dictionary, which has simplified descriptions and plenty of illustrations. Another approach that sometimes works for stubborn children is to provide them with an electronic dictionary. There are a number of battery-powered devices on the market for a reasonable price, with simplified entries and even games to play. Since most kids love gadgetry, this approach may be enough to encourage them to start looking up words.

There are other things your children can do to increase their comprehension. You should encourage them to read everything in the book, including all the picture captions, graphs, charts, and tables. Many students have a tendency to skip over graphic aids, perhaps assuming that the material is superfluous and was placed in the textbook to take up space. Emphasize to children that this material was presented by the author for a very good reason, and that they may be missing something crucial if they ignore it. It is sometimes easier for children to see and remember a relationship from a graphic aid than from the written text.

You should also realize that even if your child had read and looked at everything in a book, the author's message occasionally may not be discernible. Sometimes the ideas and principles presented in children's books can be quite complex, even if the author has made an attempt to simplify them. In such cases, your child may have to reread the material to grasp the author's message. One approach you can suggest to your child is to read the material more slowly, concentrating on one sentence at a time. There is some wonderful advice by William Walker in his book *The Art of Reading*, "Learn to read slow: all other graces, will follow in their proper places."

Here is some advice you can give to your child: After you read a sentence, pause and ask yourself what the sentence means before reading the next sentence. Encourage your child to relate new ideas to what the author has already covered. If he still cannot fully understand the concept, tell him to mark the page and skip over it temporarily. After he has read further he can refer back to this passage, and there is a good chance that he will be able to comprehend it. Sometimes it is easier to absorb ideas in the context of others in the book, just as it is easier to understand the meaning of words by viewing them within the context of other words in a sentence.

You can tell if your child has become an active reader when your youngster uses all of his or her faculties and senses to master the material. As noted earlier, different people use different senses for mastering material, and these tendencies are evident even in small children. Some learn best through their sense of sight, others through hearing, and still others find physical movement most effective. For example, some children will learn the most by reading silently. Others find that reading out loud increases their comprehension, and still others discover that writing out notes after reading is the only way to gain mastery. We often see students using a magic marker or pencil as they read, underlining key words, highlighting main ideas, writing down questions in the margins, and so on. In most instances, people use some combination of their senses to learn new material. The challenge is to help children find the combination that works best for them.

The real indication that your child is becoming a more active reader is his or her ability to anticipate the author's next thought or statement before even reading it. This indicates that your child has discerned the author's purpose, and has aligned his or her thoughts with the author's. If you are reading with your child, you can prompt this kind of thinking by asking your child, "Now what do you think the author will say next?" When children come up with the right answer they are proud of their accomplishment, and even if they fail you have stimulated their curiosity to find out what is coming next. It's a win-win situation!

Reading Faster

Notwithstanding the merits of reading slower for better comprehension, everyone wants to read faster. I would be remiss if I did not say at least something about the value of increasing reading speed. Children want to be able to read faster because time is scarce and there are plenty of other competing activities, including sports, recreation with friends, or reading other books. It is acceptable to increase reading speed, as long as a child does not do it to the exclusion of comprehension.

There has been more nonsense written about speed reading than about quack cures for cancer. You have probably seen the advertisements that promise you will be able to read the Old Testament of the Bible in three hours by running your finger down the pages in a zig-zag fashion. Scanning a page like this may be a good way to locate an entry in the telephone book, but it is not the way to become an active reader. The sad fact is that most of the people who emphasize speed are more interested in turning pages so they can tell their friends how many books they have read. Never encourage children to read so fast that they cannot understand what they have read, because the effort will have no benefit.

The processes involved in reading rapidly are relatively straightforward, whether for adults or for children. The key to rapid reading is the number of words readers can see and understand as their eyes move across the page. Children who can see a full word at a time can read more rapidly than those who have to read a single letter. And children who can see several words in a phrase at a glance will naturally read faster than those who can see only a word at a time. When children read a book, their eyes move across the page in several stops, called fixations. The more words they can see before stopping, the faster they will read.

The additional value of children looking up words in the dictionary should now be very clear. If a child's vocabulary is limited, he or she will not be able to read at a rapid and smooth rate. Every time children encounter an unfamiliar word, they must stop abruptly while they try to discern the meaning of the word. Although it may take them more time to look up words, their reading speed should increase in the long run because they will be able to read with fewer interruptions. When you explain this to children, they sometimes become more willing to look up unfamiliar words in the dictionary.

Your child should also understand that different books can be read at different rates of speed, depending upon their complexity. If youngsters read a relatively simple novel, they can do so quickly and easily because they can digest the material as fast as they encounter it. On the other hand, if they read a relatively complex mathematics or science textbook, they must obviously progress more slowly because it takes more time to study and ponder the concepts presented. However, reading assignments tend to be shorter in the more technical subjects.

As children gain more experience, they will develop a facility for reading faster. Parents should always emphasize that children need to read all of the words in a passage rather than skipping over some; otherwise, they may not fully understand the author's message. Never force children to read at a faster rate than they can handle, because they will find the experience unpleasant, which could lead to anxiety or cause their eyes to tire unnecessarily. Rather than your consciously worrying about children's reading speed, I would encourage you to help them adjust their reading speed naturally to the rate that allows them to grasp the material in a comfortable manner.

You should now have a good idea of approaches you can use to help your child become an active reader. If you can turn your child into an active reader, what used to be a humdrum chore will become an exciting new adventure. The active reader is like an explorer venturing into uncharted areas in search of knowledge and wisdom. If children enter this adventure with an open and enthusiastic mind, they will find the search interesting and exciting. Youngsters derive satisfaction from finishing a book and making it part of their own wisdom. With experience, they will look forward to reading even more books in the future.

In the interest of becoming active readers, you and your child may want to preview this entire book and read the remaining material using the principles discussed in this chapter.

Remember . . .

Principle 1
To help your children become active readers, show them how to preview a book before reading it, and ask questions that lead to a full understanding of the author's message.

2

Writing

Earlier I quoted Thomas Carlyle on the merits of reading. Carlyle also had this to say about writing: "Certainly the Age of Writing is the most miraculous of all things man has devised." Writing allows us to express our innermost thoughts in a precise way, so we can communicate them to a broad audience or preserve them for posterity. It is the principal mechanism by which we share our knowledge and feeling with others. The written word in its various forms—among them literature, history, and scientific and technical works—is the mainspring of human development and progress. The accumulation of written material provides a foundation and record of human knowledge. Without writing, there could be nothing to read, and human knowledge would have no more permanence than the passing wind.

It is important to let children know at a very early age that, as a form of communication, writing is just as essential in our society as speaking. Many of our everyday activities involve writing of some kind, whether it is the report your child writes at school, the memorandum you compose at work, or the notes you exchange with each other. Children are required to write more and more as they pass through the educational system, and for many jobs in the working world they will be required to use that skill even more extensively, because much of the communication in business is written rather than verbal, in order to provide a permanent record of events.

If we think about it carefully, there is probably not one day in our lives when we or our children have written nothing. Since writing is such an important part of our lives, doesn't it make sense to learn how to do it properly?

Writing is the most important form of communication your child will have with teachers in school—not only in English, but in all of their courses. The grade your child receives in a class is often determined largely by what he writes on examinations. In addition, many of the classes he takes will have other written assignments, such as essays, reports, themes, book reviews, and term papers. Next to reading, writing will probably demand more of your child's time as a student than any other activity.

Despite the importance of writing in our society, the skill is not well developed in the general population. Many adults in the working world cannot write well, and this is a serious obstacle to their advancement. And many high-school and college students have a negative attitude about writing because it is difficult for them. One of their major problems is that they never learned the basic principles of composition in elementary and junior high school. Plenty of people have already given up, concluding that they just cannot write well. The principles of writing I will present here will help prevent your child from becoming one of those people. This material is intended to supplement the principles of composition they will study in school.

Teaching Your Child How to Write

When learning how to write, children go through a basic process that starts with the first time they pick up a pencil and make a scribble on a piece of paper. At first this scribble may be unrecognizable, but, with time and practice, children eventually learn to favor a particular hand and the markings become more discernible and varied. Lines are vertical, horizontal, and diagonal. Circular motions exhibit both clockwise and counter-clockwise directions. Through practice parents can help their children learn the essential markings required to write the letters in the alphabet. The child will join these letters together to form simple words and, in turn, join words together to form simple sentences. In the early stages the sentences reflect incomplete thoughts, mis-spelled words, and improper grammar—but it is a start.

As your child's partner in learning, you should be there to facilitate the process of writing. You might start with assistance in the proper way to hold the writing instrument; many people learn improper methods when young that have to be unlearned later on. Or you might continue to assist your child with forming the letters of the alphabet, learning the proper relationship between capital and lower-case letters, and eventually, writing in cursive. When children write something, either at home or school, you should critique their work. Show them where they could have written more clearly, where mis-spelled words are located, where words are left out or inappropriately used, and how ideas could have been pre-sented more clearly or developed more fully. After you have provided an in-depth critique, encourage your chil-dren to make another effort to demonstrate what they have learned. Practice fed by more practice is the only means to develop genuine writing ability. You don't have to be an accomplished author to make this exercise worth-while to your child. While one learns how to write, even the most rudimentary assistance is worthwhile.

Here is a short, fun exercise that will help develop your child's writing ability. Some day when you have some extra time, tell your child a favorite story. All parents have something to relate, whether your tale is based on something that happened to you, someone else's experience, or is obtained from a book. After you have finished, ask your child to tell you a story. If he seems at a loss for words, then make some suggestions or ask him to make something up. After listening to the story, tell your child his story was so good that he should write it out for you. Give him paper and pencil, and suggest a secluded place to compose his tale. After he has finished, critique the work in the manner described above, make corrections, suggest other ideas, etc.

Then send your child back to the drawing board and ask for a rewrite. You may need to go through a couple of cycles until the work is satisfactory to both of you. Save the story in a folder so you can monitor your child's development and have a valued memento later on. I have found that children respond very readily to this exercise, because they enjoy writing a story they made up, especially when someone else is interested in it. One of the biggest roadblocks to writing is a lack of something to say.

Once children learn to read, it is easier for them to master the fine art of writing. Exposure to the written word through reading familiarizes youngsters with words. They will learn many new words, particularly if they have diligently used a dictionary. When learning how to write, children will employ the words they have seen in books. A book is a living example of how the letters of the alphabet are strung together to form words, how words are joined together to form sentences, and how sentences are grouped together to form paragraphs. Children improve upon their own ways of developing and expressing thoughts when they see how a professional author does it. The principle is no different than learning how to improve your skill at a sport by taking lessons from a professional.

Let's assume that your child has just received a writing assignment at school. It might be in the form of an essay or theme, or a longer work such as a research paper. Regardless of the kind of assignment, there are certain basic steps required for effective writing. The steps include: selecting a topic, conducting research, developing an outline, writing a first draft, and then writing a final version. If parents can get their children to follow these simple steps, they will be helping their children become more effective writers.

Selecting a Topic

Children often get writing assignments by the time they are in the first or second grade. Sometimes the teacher selects a topic for a writing assignment, and sometimes the student is allowed to choose one. Even when teachers select a topic, they usually give students at least some leeway in deciding what to write about. When children have some say in the selection of a topic, the paramount rule is that they should choose a subject they are interested in. It might be a subject that has always fascinated them, or an intriguing topic discussed by the teacher. Interest in a subject is very important because writing often requires a lot of research and effort, and the task is made easier if one approaches it willingly.

One of the biggest problems writers have—adults and children alike—is narrowing a topic down to something manageable. People have a natural tendency to take on very broad subjects, and consequently are unable to deal with them effectively in a paper or theme. Parents should encourage their children to pick a topic that is specific so they can focus their attention and effort in this direction. Make sure your child avoids topics that are general, vague, or controversial, because they may be impossible to deal with in the space and time available to write the paper. When children come up with an idea for a topic, it is best for parents to discuss it with them at length. Parents have the benefit of perspective that comes from experience, and can help their children avoid attempting more than they can manage.

Once parents have helped their children select a good topic, the next step is to get them to think about it very carefully. To do this, parents should ask children to consider the types of questions they want to answer. This should be a lengthy exercise in which children are able to discuss anything that comes to their minds. This exercise helps to focus attention on a subject and identifies issues that will need to be addressed. It is best to encourage children to come up with questions on their own, but if they hit a snag there is nothing wrong with parents suggesting additional questions. Sometimes this is all that is needed to get children thinking about a subject from a different direction. Identifying questions that need to be answered encourages curiosity, and is the first step for any type of writing. Be sure that children write down the questions they want to answer, or they may be forgotten when they conduct their research.

Conducting Research

Children are often asked to conduct research by the time they are in the third or fourth grade. Conducting research sounds like a very formal endeavor, but it doesn't have to be. Almost all writers conduct at least some research for everything they write. Your child might get a writing assignment at school for something straightforward like describing what happened during the summer vacation, which would only require a recollection of experiences. On the other hand, your youngster may be asked to write a lengthy term paper about some important historical figure or event, which would call for extensive research in the library. The important point is that some research is needed in both cases to assemble the raw material that will go into the writing effort. Let's take a closer look at what is involved if your child has been asked to write a lengthy research paper.

The starting point is your child's instructor. The instructor can direct your child toward key reading materials that relate to the topic. In some cases, teachers distribute reading lists that provide various sources of information on specific topics. If your child has such a list, but none of the suggested works seems germane, then tell your youngster to ask the teacher about other reading sources that relate to the topic. Most teachers are very receptive to inquiries of this type. Even finding a few reading sources provides a good start, because they may well include references to related reading materials.

Part of the educational experience in writing these first research papers is learning how to use the library. That is the place to locate the additional reading materials suggested by the teacher, and perhaps find some new ones as well. If you have began taking your child to the library from an early age, he or she should find it a very comfortable and welcome place. Now is the time to help your child delve more deeply into the internal workings of the library. Start by showing your youngster how to look up reading sources in the card catalogue under either the author's name or the subject matter. Explain how to read the various pieces of information on the card for each entry and, specifically, how to locate a book in the stacks by its call number. As you go through the card catalogue, you and your child will likely find other reading sources that are relevant to the topic. Write down the call numbers for all of the books you want. After you have done this together a few times, your youngsters should be prepared to do it on their own the next time.

There is one more thing you can do before visiting the book stacks. Many modern libraries have computerized bibliographic search systems for locating reading sources. Using a few key words about the subject, these systems can locate additional books and articles, not only in your library but in others as well. Many systems provide a useful printout with a summary of the content of each item, which will help your child determine if a source is relevant to the topic. In general, you should teach your child how to use the various resources in the library, including books, articles, encyclopedia and other reference books, and the librarian.

If children are now familiar with the material in the chapter on reading, they will know how to review a book to determine if it is relevant to their topic. By scanning the table of contents, summaries, and headings, they should not have to take more than a few minutes to make a determination. Parents should go through this exercise a few times until their children know what to do.

When youngsters find sources that are relevant to their topic, they should take careful notes as they read. Reading without taking notes will not be of much use, because the material will likely be forgotten long before the child starts to write the paper. Parents may need to provide assistance in recording relevant information. If children come across a passage they want to quote, then they should designate it with quotation marks, and check what they have written to make sure it is accurate. Children frequently take notes verbatim from books they are reading and put the thoughts into their own words later, while writing the paper. I think it is better for children to translate the author's thoughts into their own words while writing notes because the information will become more meaningful to them that way. In addition, they avoid the task of translation later, when the thought is not as clear. Whether children quote or translate another person's thoughts, they will need to keep track of relevant information for references and citations. Make sure that they properly record bibliographic information, such as the title of the book, name of the author, publishing house, where and when it was published, and the page number. This may seem time consuming, but it is no fun looking up these details at a later point. And do not assume that these are extraneous details, because more and more teachers require them—even at the lower grade levels.

Your child will need to have some type of system for recording all of the information collected during the research phase. Some researchers employ elaborate index card systems, using three-by-five cards for recording bibliographic information and larger cards for taking notes. I prefer to use plain notebook paper. It doesn't matter which system children use, as long as it makes them comfortable and is truly systematic. One recommendation is worth noting. Encourage youngsters to write only on one side of the page—because it is easier for them to spread everything out so they can see what they have recorded. Referring to notes can become very messy and confusing when they are written on both sides of the paper.

In all research, the objective is to come up with something new, not merely regurgitate what is already known. Although this may sound too ambitious for younger children, the teacher at least wants to see that your child can develop new thoughts from a synthesis of the various reading sources. To do so, you will need to create an environment that encourages creative thinking.

Creative thinking involves several distinct stages. The first is to recognize relevant questions clearly, which is what your child did when he or she first embarked on the research effort. The next stage is to accumulate as much knowledge as possible about the subject—to become immersed in it. This essentially is what your child did when he or she read every resource available. The next stage is for your child to leave the subject alone for a while and let it incubate in the subconscious mind. While the conscious mind may not consider the subject, the subconscious mind is busy at work, coming up with new approaches and solutions. At some point, an ingenious insight could pop into your child's head—the product of creative thinking. All your child needs to do now is compare it against the question asked in the first stage to make sure it is a good solution. Be sure children record these insights in their notes, or they may be lost forever.

As your child progresses with the research, the nature of the questions may have changed, or at least become more specific. This is a natural development, because sometimes it is impossible to come up with specific questions before doing the research. After your child has read all of the sources and refined all of the questions, it is then time to impose some structure on this mountain of material.

Developing an Outline

Before your youngster starts to write the research paper, she will be well served by an outline that helps to order thoughts. Whenever conducting research, one undoubtedly notices that the material is grouped in some logical fashion. The grouping may have been chronological, geographical, or numerical, or according to the order of importance or complexity. By putting this information into an outline, it will be easier for your child to see these logical groupings more clearly.

There is nothing particularly difficult about preparing an outline, but it is important to do so properly. Your child has probably already learned how to prepare an outline from early years at school. If not, the approach is really quite straightforward. The title of the paper should appear as the title of the outline. Major topics should be designated by Roman numerals and minor topics should be designated by capital letters, indented under the major topics. Minor topics can be subdivided further, by using Arabic numerals, small letters, and so on, all with increasing indentation. When organized in this fashion, the outline serves as a blueprint to guide the structure and pattern of your child's thoughts. The outline will help your child to see the arrangement of the material, to check the balance between major and minor topics, as well as repetitions and contradictions, and to facilitate the development and expression of new ideas.

After your child has produced the outline, which sometimes takes time to put together, you will need to show your youngster how to flesh it out. The idea is to index all the notes from the readings to specific parts of the outline. In other words, have your child write the number or letter of the corresponding topic from the outline on the appropriate pages of notes from the readings. Your child is now ready to write a first draft.

Writing a First Draft

One of the most difficult parts of writing a paper for most people is getting started. Some people despise writing so much that they will look for any excuse to procrastinate. They complain of writer's block or some other problem. Parents can help children overcome this obstacle by encouraging them to sit down at their desk or typewriter, get out their outline and notes, take out some blank paper, and *start writing!* Once they get started, things should flow more smoothly.

As a general guide to good writing, encourage your child to structure the paper with a beginning, middle, and end.

The beginning, or introduction, of the paper is important because that is where your child will state the central theme and attempt to encourage the reader to continue reading. Instruct children that a lengthy introduction is unnecessary; a successful introduction is brief and makes the reader eager to get into the body of the paper. Just because the introduction will be short does not mean that it will be easy. It can be very difficult to write a good introduction before actually writing the body of the text; indeed some writers argue that the introduction should be written last, after the author sees how the paper has turned out. But I think it is best to compose the introduction at the outset. Even if your child has to redo the introduction several times, he or she will at least have the material for working on different approaches.

In order to write the middle, or body, of the paper, all your child has to do is to merge notes from the readings into the outline. The major topics in the outline become the chapters or major headings in the paper. The minor topics in the outline become minor headings within the chapters or under the major headings. The notes from the readings flesh out the body of the paper under each heading. The major and minor headings should stand out and display the proper hierarchical order. Teaching a child how to approach writing in a methodical way results in a more enjoyable experience and a better product.

I do not plan to review all of the *fundamentals* of good writing here—after all, that is why children take English courses throughout most of their academic career. I will, however, mention a few of the major points required for good paragraph construction. Show your child how the first or second sentence, known as the topic sentence, states the major idea of the paragraph. Then illustrate how to use additional sentences to support the point through the use of facts, examples, statistics, and so on. It is important to give the reader some concrete evidence to support the point being made. The paragraphs should be presented in a logical fashion to develop the theme, just like the telling of a story. Many children tend to write in a stilted fashion. Parents need to show them how to add transitions between the sentences and paragraphs so the presentation flows smoothly. In addition, parents also should explain how to vary the length of paragraphs, and sentences within paragraphs, so the writing will not become monotonous. All the details on the proper use of words, such as the various parts of speech, can be found in your child's schoolbooks on English grammar and composition.

When writing the end of the paper, your child should include a conclusion that summarizes the major findings. The conclusion should refer back to the introduction and address any important issues raised there. The conclusion should also cast the findings in a broader light in terms of their implications, and the need and direction of further research. This may seem to be a tall order for a child, but teachers look for this approach. The most important point is that the conclusion contains the final thought your child will leave with the reader.

Encourage children to try to make the first draft of the paper as close to the final product as possible, to keep down the amount of revision. This will require vigilance on the part of parents as the effort progresses. Make sure youngsters observe the proper mechanics of writing in the construction of paragraphs and sentences and that they use correct spelling. They should put citations in the appropriate places. You may find that when children write at a fairly rapid rate the result will be a smoother, more even-flowing version that will be closer to the desired final product.

After your child finishes the first draft, put the work aside and let it sit for a while. This lapse of time should help your child come up with new ideas or approaches that will strengthen the presentation. It is very important to observe this short wait. Do not try to bypass it. Afterward, your child should be ready to write the final version.

Writing the Final Version

I know what your child will be thinking and saying: "After all of this work I have to write another version. It isn't fair." They thought they were finished. Even though the first version may have looked very good initially, you and she will undoubtedly see many flaws after a careful inspection at a later date. Even accomplished writers occasionally find it difficult to write polished prose. Dale Carnegie, author of one of the most popular books ever written, used to say, "It is easier to make a million dollars than to put a phrase into the English language." And Mr. Carnegie ought to know, because his book, *How to Win Friends & Influence People*, sold millions of copies and made millions of dollars—in addition to adding a phrase to the English language.

Most writers dislike the task of rewriting, but it makes the difference between a rough and a finished product. You can explain the effort to your child by comparing it to the process an artist goes through in painting a picture. (This should be a good analogy for children to understand.) The artist painting a landscape first lays out basic forms such as the sky, mountains, and rivers. We can recognize these basic shapes at this stage, but the painting is far from finished. Next the artist begins to fill in some of the details, and the shapes can be discerned more clearly. The artist continues to add detail until the painting embodies the desired effect.

As with the painting, your child may have to rewrite the paper several times until he or she is satisfied. During this process, your child will eliminate unnecessary text, sharpen the language, improve the flow of ideas, and refine the introduction and conclusion, among other things. If your child approaches this stage seriously, the eraser should be almost as busy as the pencil. Since this is an unfamiliar process to most children, parents should be there to help with guidance and advice. It is best to begin as soon as children get their first writing assignment.

When children write their final version, parents should make sure they adhere to all of the basic style conventions. They should produce a neat product on standard-size (8-1/2 by 11 inches) white paper, with adequate margins on all four sides. Students should use the appropriate conventions for making citations and references, and follow these conventions consistently throughout the entire paper. There are any number of good style manuals on the market. One I like that is not too advanced for students if parents provide assistance is, Kate L. Turabian, *Students's Guide for Writing College Papers*. I think it is best for students to learn the same style conventions that will be required later on, so they do not have to unlearn what they already know.

Some teachers have their own conventions and, if this is the case, they usually communicate this information to their students at an early stage. If the teacher wants footnotes and references cited a certain way, make sure your child does so. If the teacher asks students to use a certain size paper and to type the results, make sure your child does what is expected. These are small concessions to make and could result in a significantly higher grade.

Some Final Words of Advice

In order to complete all of the steps I have outlined, it is very important that children begin work on their writing assignment as soon as possible. There are no hard and fast rules about the amount of time a youngster should devote to each of the steps. As a general rule, I suggest that children spend about one-half of their time selecting a topic, raising relevant questions, and conducting research on the various sources. This leaves the remaining time for developing an outline, writing a first draft, and writing the final version. It is important to explain to children that if they do not begin their work early, they will not have enough time to complete each of the steps. They will need all of the time they can get to think creatively, come up with some new ideas, and write a polished paper.

Students tend to procrastinate on writing assignments, and often end up hating the whole affair. I know, because I was one of the worst offenders throughout many of my years in school. I often produced shoddy work and rarely met the deadline for completing the task. Now I spend much of my time writing and enjoy doing so. I start to write soon after I have a contract for a book, and maintain the momentum throughout the process. This enables me to proceed with my work at a leisurely pace. Often the way for children to get around an aversion to writing is to sit down and get started, and then everything begins to flow naturally. If your child complains of something akin to writer's block, the best approach is to make your youngster sit at a desk and start moving the pen.

My discussion in this chapter has focused on the steps needed to write a full-scale research paper, because this is the most complicated, challenging writing assignment a youngster is likely to be given. If children know how to tackle the research paper, they will know how to handle every other writing assignment as well. All writing assignments call for the same basic steps; the only difference is that the amount of time required for each step varies for essays, themes, and full-scale papers. Children will have many writing mentors over time, but their most important mentors may be their parents. After all, parents are continuously there to help their youngsters progress from writing the first scribbles on paper to the point where they can compose polished prose.

It takes a lot of time and practice to develop skill in writing, but it is an investment that will yield a good return over an entire lifetime. If you want your child to develop into a first-rate writer, you must make sure that he or she follows . . .

Principle 2
To write a good paper, select a topic, think up relevant questions, conduct research, develop an outline, then write and rewrite as necessary. Start early!

3

Arithmetic

Galileo, the great Italian physicist and astronomer, had this to say about the universe: "It is written in the language of mathematics, and its characters are triangles, circles, and other geometrical figures, without which it is humanly impossible to understand a single word of it; without these, one is wandering about in a dark labyrinth."

With no knowledge of mathematics, that is exactly where your child will be—wandering about in a dark labyrinth. To their own detriment, many people make no effort to learn mathematics. I know, because as a young student I was one of the worst offenders.

Although many years have since passed, I can vividly remember entering my high-school trigonometry class the day of a big test. I had that queasy feeling in my stomach, my knees were limp, and my heart was beating so rapidly in my throat that I could hardly breathe. I had not really understood any of the material covered in the book or presented in class. When I opened the exam paper it looked like Greek; in fact, many of the symbols were in Greek. I suffered through that hour with a constant stream of sweat running down my brow, guessing wildly in the hope that I might get lucky. When the teacher

74

returned the test paper, it only confirmed what I already knew. I received an F. And when I was given my report card at the end of the semester I was not surprised to discover that I had flunked the course. I hated math more than anything in the world.

My aversion continued into college. Looking at the course curriculum I remember shuddering when I read that economics majors were *required* to take a certain amount of math in order to graduate. I was not alone in my fear. Some business majors were terrified at the thought of taking math. "Don't worry," the physics and math majors assured us. "With the cookbook courses you're taking it will be a piece of cake." Well, it wasn't. Sheer hell would be a more accurate description. Multicolored balls emerging out of urns, funny-looking Greek symbols with misplaced numerals, and confounding lines drawn all over graphs. I was more confused than ever. But I knew that I had to master this subject if I hoped to graduate. With all of my efforts I managed to scrape by with a D. I was also able to get through two more math courses and complete my graduation requirement.

After graduation I went back to college at night, this time to take math courses with the physics and math majors. I was now prepared for the challenge. I had learned some theory, had a lot of good practical experience, and knew I would study differently. I was still scared, but I had developed a system that worked like a charm. I took all of the difficult math courses—differential calculus, integral calculus, linear algebra, calculus of several variables—and then went on to take mathematical statistics. Afterward I earned a Ph.D. in economics, taking difficult quantitative courses like mathematical economics, econometrics, and operations research. During my "second" college career I made an A not only in every course but on every exam. And to my surprise making A's in math was easy to achieve.

What did I learn from all of these experiences—most important, what is the lesson for your own child? How can you prevent your youngster from experiencing all of this misery? The answer, simply, is that you have to help develop an appreciation and understanding of mathematics in children by introducing concepts to them in a very methodical and progressive manner. Let me give you one more example of what I have in mind.

The first math teacher I encountered on my second return to college was one of the most proficient teachers I ever had. When teaching us differential calculus, he would start at the beginning and state the obvious. What he said was so obvious that several of us in the class looked at each other and wondered why he would say something that was almost common sense. We continued to feel this way throughout the entire semester since everything he said followed so clearly from what he had said before. By the end of the semester we were amazed at how much we had learned when we glanced back through our textbook. And it had all been so painless, even fun. This is the same type of approach that you should use in helping your child to have an understanding and appreciation of mathematics.

In what follows I will not present a lot of rigorous and detailed mathematical concepts. In my next book, *Math Made Simple*, I plan to present a whole series of mathematical concepts, up to and including higher mathematics, in a manner that anyone can understand. In this chapter I will cover the basic mathematical concepts that elementary- and junior-high-school students should know in order to have a good grasp of the subject. In the process, I will be offering tips to parents on how they can help their children master these concepts in a logical and painless fashion. The object is to develop a good foundation that will support further growth in mathematics later on, in a manner that shows children just how much fun mathematics can be.

Basic Arithmetic

The starting point for an understanding of mathematics is mastery of the basic concept of counting. We typically start our children at a very young age by teaching them counting rules on our fingers. This is how they learn to associate numbers with things, like fingers, and begin to realize that larger numbers signify more of something than smaller numbers. Gradually we teach our youngsters that counting rules apply to any discrete item, and that the number of such items can be much larger than the number of fingers we possess. Eventually, we teach them the positions in which a number can be represented—ones, tens, hundreds, thousands, etc.—and then show them how large numbers are divided into groups of three digits separated by commas.

Soon after children learn how to count, we introduce them to basic arithmetic such as addition and subtraction. We start with small numbers, again usually fingers, and explain that adding two numbers yields another number called a sum, and that subtracting one number from that sum gets us back to the other number. We should also be teaching our children certain basic properties of addition, such as:

Commutative Property
If the order of numbers
    added together is changed, $2 + 5 = 5 + 2$
    the result (sum) stays the same $7 = 7$

Identity Property

If zero is added to any number,	$4 + 0 = 4$
the sum is equal to the number.	$0 + 8 = 8$

Associative Property

If the grouping of numbers is changed, $(1 + 6) + 9 = 1 + (6 + 9)$
the sum remains the same.   ↓   ↓

$$7 + 9 = 1 + \quad 15$$
$$16 = 16$$

In a similar manner, we should teach our children the properties of subtraction, such as:

If zero is subtracted from any number,	$4 - 0 = 4$
the result (difference) is just the number.	$7 - 0 = 7$

When any number is subtracted from itself,	$5 - 5 = 0$
the difference is always zero.	$8 - 8 = 0$

Subtraction, unlike addition,	$9 - 3 = 6$
is not commutative.	$3 - 9 \neq 6$

(where $\neq$ means *not equal to*)

Once children learn the basic operations of addition and subtraction, they can progress to more difficult tasks such as adding and subtracting large numbers. This may involve adding several large numbers together, and knowing how to carry over the sum from one column to another. It may also involve the subtraction of one large number from an even larger one, and knowing how to borrow from an adjacent column.

Of course, the real test of an understanding of addition and subtraction is the ability to read a word problem and express it mathematically. Children will have plenty of opportunity in school to solve word problems, and they usually have much more difficulty doing this than performing routine arithmetical operations. For this reason, parents should give their children plenty of practice solving word problems from their early years. Word problems can involve simple little games and puzzles using objects, people, or money. The objective is to give children experience in translating verbal and written descriptions into mathematical representations, so they will not be intimidated when they encounter more difficult word problems later on.

Once children become comfortable with the concepts of addition and subtraction, it is time to introduce them to multiplication and division. To help in making the transition, we should note that addition is related to multiplication in that adding the same number to itself several times is the same as multiplying the number by that number of times. Of course, the best way to teach multiplication and division is through the familiar multiplication tables.

I am of the old school that believes children should do an adequate amount of work to memorize their "times tables," all the way up to the number twelve. Parents can start out by helping children to memorize certain facts, such as what is one times one, one times two, one times three, and so on, all the way up to twelve times twelve. The process is facilitated by laying out the multiplication table, with the numbers one through twelve running down the side of the page, the numbers one through twelve running across the top of the page, and a grid with each box containing the product of the two numbers that form its intersection. The multiplication table is a useful device that enables children to memorize the various products of numbers. It also allows children to see that division is the opposite of multiplication, since the product divided by one of the numbers equals the other number. I have included a times table in an appendix that you can use to practice with your youngster.

In the process of teaching children how to multiply and divide, it is important to explain to them the basic properties of multiplication and division. Here are some basic properties of multiplication:

Multiplication Properties

Identity Property

If one of the factors is 1, the
product equals the other factor. $4 \times 1 = 4$ $1 \times 5 = 5$

Zero Property

If one of the factors is 0, the
product equals 0. $7 \times 0 = 0$ $0 \times 8 = 0$

Commutative Property

If factors are multiplied in a
different order, the product is $6 \times 9 = 54$ $9 \times 6 = 54$
still the same.

Associative Property

If the factors are grouped together $(3 \times 4) \times 5 = 3 \times (4 \times 5)$
differently, the product is still   ↓   ↓
the same. $12 \times 5 = 3 \times 20$
                                                      $60 = 60$

Distributive Property

To multiply a factor by the sum $6 \times (7 + 8) = (6 \times 7) + (6 \times 8)$
of two numbers, multiply the   ↓   ↓   ↓
factor by each number separately, $6 \times 15 = 42 + 48$
and then add the two products. $90 = 90$

The basic properties of division are equally straightforward:

Division Properties

When any number is divided by 1, $4 \div 1 = 4$
the result is equal to the number.

When any number (except 0) is divided by itself, the result is equal to 1.	$6 \div 6 = 1$
Division of a number by 0 is not allowed. (If $8 \div 0$ = some number n, then $n \times 0$ = 8—which doesn't make sense.)	$8 \div 0$ not defined
When 0 is divided by another number (except 0), the result is 0.	$0 \div 7 = 0$

If children learn these basic properties of multiplication and division, they will have an easier time later on with more complex problems, such as word problems or multiplication and division by multiple-digit numbers. Youngsters will get plenty of practice with these concepts at school, but it helps if parents can offer additional tutoring at home. For example, parents can show their children how to multiply a number by another number that is two digits, three digits, or larger. It is important to explain how one carries the product of each multiplication to an adjacent column, and how to stack the resulting rows so they can be added to get the correct result.

With division, it is important to explain how one divides by multiple-digit numbers, and how to handle remainders. Parents should also show their children how to check the results of their division (quotient times divisor equals the dividend). With both multiplication and division, operations involving zero are special cases, and these should be covered as well.

Since these mechanics are just tools, the real test of their mastery comes from being able to interpret a word problem correctly and set it up as a mathematical expression. This is where parents can be particularly helpful in mastering the concepts involved.

As children develop a facility for arithmetic, they will realize that there are shorthand methods for deriving results. For example, by rounding and estimating, it is possible to determine an approximate result quickly. And, of course, if a calculator or home computer is used, an exact result can be derived almost immediately. While these approaches are often used by adults, and eventually by their children, there is no substitute for learning how to do arithmetic the old-fashioned way. Knowledge of basic arithmetic forms the only solid foundation for understanding more complex operations later on.

Fractions and Decimals

All of the discussion on arithmetic thus far has involved whole numbers, but children also need to be introduced to the concepts of fractions and decimals. All parents probably introduce their children to the concept of fractions at an early age. For example, a parent slicing a whole pie might explain to a child that if a pie is cut into four equal pieces then each piece is a fourth. Also, each fourth can be cut in half, so now there are eight pieces, each representing an eighth, and so on. We formalize the concept when we explain to children that a fraction is represented by a numerator (the number of sliced pieces) divided by a denominator (the total number of pieces). We extend the concept further when we explain that one-fourth of the pie is an equivalent fraction to two-eighths of the pie.

There are several basic concepts that children need to know about fractions. Perhaps the most basic is that if we divide or multiply both the numerator and denominator of a fraction by a common factor (number), the value of the fraction is unchanged. For example, to express a fraction in its simplest form, all we need to do is divide both the numerator and denominator by the largest common factor:

$$\frac{16}{20} = \frac{16 \div 4}{20 \div 4} = \frac{4}{5} \qquad\qquad \frac{18}{24} = \frac{18 \div 6}{24 \div 6} = \frac{3}{4}$$

In another basic concept, quantities are sometimes represented by mixed numbers, which include both a whole number and a fraction. Children need to know how to multiply the denominator of the fraction by the whole number and then add it to the numerator to change the mixed number back to an ordinary fraction, and vice versa:

$$2\frac{3}{4} = \frac{(2 \times 4) + 3}{4} = \frac{11}{4} \qquad \text{and} \qquad \frac{11}{4} = 11 \div 4 = 2\frac{3}{4}$$

They also need to know how to convert two or more fractions to a common denominator to determine which is larger. And, of course, converting to a common base (denominator) will enable them to add and subtract fractions. A special case involves adding and subtracting mixed numbers. If children have learned the proper way to add and subtract from basic arithmetic, all they are doing is extending the concept to apply to fractions:

$$\frac{2}{9} = \frac{2 \times 2}{9 \times 2} = \frac{4}{18} \qquad\qquad 4\frac{5}{8} = 4\frac{15}{24}$$

$$+\ \frac{1}{6} = \frac{1 \times 3}{6 \times 3} = \frac{3}{18} \qquad\qquad -\ 2\frac{1}{3} = 2\frac{8}{24}$$

$$\frac{7}{18} \qquad\qquad\qquad\qquad 2\frac{7}{24}$$

In a similar manner, if children have learned how to multiply and divide properly from basic arithmetic, it is a simple matter to extend their knowledge to fractions. Parents need to show children that they do not have to convert to a common denominator to multiply two fractions; all they need to do is to multiply the two numerators together to form a new numerator, and multiply the two denominators together to form a new denominator. Of course, the resulting fraction may not be in its simplest form, but children now know how to express the fraction in its simplest form. Parents should emphasize to their children that all they are doing is applying something they already know, which is always easier than learning something totally new.

$$\frac{8}{9} \times \frac{3}{4} = \frac{8 \times 3}{9 \times 4} = \frac{24}{36} = \frac{2}{3}$$

Another good example is multiplying mixed numbers and ordinary fractions together; all they have to do is make the proper conversion before carrying out the multiplication. You can also show your child how to save a step by dividing numerators and denominators that are divisible:

$$6\frac{1}{2} \times \frac{2}{3} = \frac{13}{\cancel{2}_{1}} \times \frac{\cancel{2}^{1}}{3} = \frac{13}{3}$$

And, so division of fractions will not seem like something totally new, all parents need to mention is that to divide by a fraction we only need to take its reciprocal (invert it) and then proceed as if we are multiplying by it. All of the rules of multiplication still apply.

$$8\frac{1}{2} \div \frac{5}{8} = \frac{17}{2} \div \frac{5}{8} = \frac{17}{\cancel{2}_{1}} \times \frac{\cancel{8}^{4}}{5} = \frac{68}{5} = 13\frac{3}{5}$$

Once children understand fractions, it is a simple matter for them to understand decimals. All parents need to do is explain that if the denominator of a fraction is divided into the numerator, the result is a decimal. It is a simple matter to show them where to place the decimal point, and how to read different number positions such as tenths, hundredths, thousandths, and so on. All of the rules of addition and subtraction apply, as long as they know where to place the decimal point.

$$
\begin{array}{r}
5\,6.2\,9\,4 \\
+\ 4\,7.4\,8\,9 \\
\hline
1\,0\,3.7\,8\,3
\end{array}
\qquad
\begin{array}{r}
4\,8.3\,6\,1 \\
-\ 3\,9.2\,7\,4 \\
\hline
9.0\,8\,7
\end{array}
$$

The same applies to multiplication, once children know how to count up the number of decimal places in the numbers being multiplied, and reflect the result in the product. And, of course, with division involving decimals, all they need to do is shift the decimal point in the divisor all the way to the right, and shift the decimal in the dividend by the same number of places. All of the other rules of multiplication and division apply, just as before:

$$
\begin{array}{r}
1.9\,5 \\
\times\ \ 2\,2.5 \\
\hline
9\,7\,5 \\
3\,9\,0 \\
3\,9\,0 \\
\hline
4\,3.8\,7\,5
\end{array}
\qquad
\begin{array}{r}
5\,6. \\
8\,4\,)\overline{4\,7,0\,4} \\
4\,2\,0 \\
\hline
5\,0\,4 \\
5\,0\,4 \\
\hline
0
\end{array}
$$

Once children understand how to work with fractions and decimals, it is easy for them to understand ratios, proportions, and percents. A ratio is just a way of comparing two related numbers that can be expressed as a fraction or a rate; for example, the fraction two-fifths can be expressed as two to five or two:five. When we have equal ratios, we say that they are a proportion. A percent is a ratio that compares some number to a hundred. Again, nothing new, just an extension of what children already know. Here are examples of each:

Ratio	Proportion	Percent
2 to 5		
$\frac{2}{5}$ means or	$\frac{2}{5} = \frac{8}{20}$	$\frac{2}{5} = \frac{40}{100} = 40\%$
2 out of 5		

Weights and Measures

All parents teach their children the basic concepts of weights and measures from a very early age. One of the first things children learn about are the customary units of time, such as minutes, hours, days, weeks, years, and centuries. Parents can help in these efforts by showing children how these units are expressed on a clock or calendar. Around the same time, children also learn about temperature, although usually using the familiar Fahrenheit scale rather than the Celsius scale that is often employed in scientific work. Parents assist in these efforts by introducing their children to a thermometer, and showing them how the scale corresponds to different temperatures ranging from cold to hot.

Children also learn about the customary units of length—such as inches, feet, yards, and miles—and how they relate to each other. Here again, parents can help their youngsters master these concepts by demonstrating sample units of length using either a ruler or yardstick. And finally, children learn about the customary units of capacity and weight from an early age. Thus, they learn that liquid volumes can be measured by cups, pints, quarts, and gallons, and that weight can be measured by ounces, pounds, and tons. Parents can also help by showing their children sample units of capacity, by pouring liquid into containers, and sample units of weight, by using an ordinary bathroom or kitchen scale. In all of these efforts, it helps if parents create word problems requiring conversion between the various units of weights and measures and arithmetic operations involving them.

With time and practice, almost all children learn about the customary weights and measures used in the United States. The real problem often comes when children are required to learn about metric weights and measures in school. The problem arises because children are confronted with measures that are not often used in their daily lives, and many parents have difficulty describing these concepts because they were never taught them in school. An understanding of metric units is essential for any child in today's world because these concepts are used universally in scientific work and in most of the rest of the world. Eventually they will be used throughout the United States. Moreover, these concepts are easier to work with than our customary units of weights and measures, because they are expressed in multiples of ten.

Metric weights and measures are similar in concept to the ones we are already familiar with, only they are expressed on a different scale. We will start off with the basic metric measure of *length*, which is the meter. The meter is a little more than one yard long. This is easy enough to understand, but the difficulty usually comes when trying to understand and remember the various measures related to the meter. Ranging from largest to smallest, they are the kilometer (km), hectometer (hm), dekameter (dam), meter (m), decimeter (dm), centimeter (cm), and millimeter (mm). A kilometer is one thousand times as large as a meter, and a millimeter is one-thousandth of a meter; the other measures decrease by a factor of ten from largest to smallest. An easy way for children to remember this progression is through the saying: *King Henry Died Monday Drinking Chocolate Milk*, where the first letter of each word in the sentence refers to the first letter of metric lengths from largest (kilometer) to smallest (millimeter):

King	Henry	Died	Monday	Drinking	Chocolate	Milk
km	hm	dam	m	dm	cm	mm
kilometer	hectometer	dekameter	meter	decimeter	centimeter	millimeter
1km	1hm	1dam		10dm	100cm	1,000mm
= 1,000m	= 100m	= 10m		= 1m	= 1m	= 1m

The metric unit of *capacity* is the liter. A liter is a little more than a quart. The various measures related to the liter, ranging from largest to smallest, are the kiloliter (kl), hectoliter (hl), dekaliter (dal), liter (l) deciliter (dl), centiliter (cl), and milliliter (ml). A kiloliter is one thousand times as large as a liter, and a milliliter is one-thousandth of a liter; as before, the other measures decrease by a factor of ten from largest to smallest. To help children remember this progression, we can change the popular saying to: *King Henry Died Later Drinking Chocolate Milk*, where the first letter of each word refers to the first letter of metric capacities from largest (kiloliter) to smallest (milliliter):

King	Henry	Died	Later	Drinking	Chocolate	Milk
kl	hl	dal	l	dl	cl	ml
kiloliter	hectoliter	dekaliter	liter	deciliter	centiliter	milliliter
1kl	1hl	1dal		10dl	100cl	1,000ml
= 1,000l	= 100l	= 10l		= 1l	= 1l	= 1l

The final metric measure we will consider is that of *mass*, which is the amount of matter contained in an object. The metric unit of mass is the gram. A gram is only a fraction of an ounce (.035 ounce). The various measures related to the gram, ranging from largest to smallest, are the kilogram (kg), hectogram (hg), dekagram (dag), gram (g), decigram (dg), centigram (cg), and milligram (mg). A kilogram is one thousand times as large as a gram, and a milligram is one-thousandth of a gram; again, the other measures decrease by a factor of ten from largest to smallest. As a way to remember them, we will change the saying to: *K*ing *H*enry *D*ied *G*hastly *D*rinking *C*hocolate *M*ilk, where the first letter of each word refers to the first letter of metric masses from largest (kilogram) to smallest (milligram):

King	Henry	Died	Ghastly	Drinking	Chocolate	Milk
kg	hg	dag	g	dg	cg	mg
kilogram	hectogram	dekagram	gram	decigram	centigram	milligram
1kg	1hg	1dag		10dg	100cg	1,000mg
= 1,000g	= 100g	= 10g		= 1g	= 1g	= 1g

In helping children to learn these metric measures, it is important for parents to work closely and patiently with them. Again, the technique of devising word problems that require conversion and arithmetical operations is good advice here.

Geometry

Although plane and solid geometry are usually taught after a course in algebra in junior high or high school, children typically encounter geometrical concepts while they are still in elementary school. For this reason, I will discuss geometry before algebra.

The word geometry is derived from an ancient Greek word that means "to measure the earth." With geometry, the student moves from the world of numbers to the world of physical representation. As such, the student will be introduced to concepts such as points, lines, rays, line segments, angles, and planes. These are the building blocks that are used to construct the geometrical figures that we usually associate with the word *geometry*. The starting point is an understanding of different types of lines, such as parallel, perpendicular, and other intersecting lines. From this understanding, children can see that intersecting lines form a variety of angles, such as straight (180°), right (90°), obtuse (between 90° and 180°), and acute (less than 90°) angles. It is good practice for children to construct a variety of angles and then measure them with a protractor.

Once children understand lines and angles, it becomes much easier for them to comprehend how geometrical figures are constructed. Perhaps the most important geometrical figure is the triangle, and it receives a lot of emphasis later on in plane geometry. Children should be introduced early to the different types of triangles classified by the length of their sides, such as equilateral (all sides equal), isosceles (two sides equal), and scalene (no sides equal):

Equilateral triangle	Isosceles triangle	Scalene triangle
All sides are equal.	At least two sides are equal.	No sides are equal.

Alternatively they should become familiar with different types of triangles based on their angles, such as acute (three acute angles), right (one right angle), and obtuse (one obtuse angle). Even young children should know that the sum of the measures of angles in a triangle is 180°.

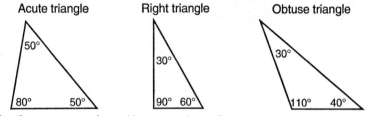

Acute triangle
50°
80°   50°
Has three acute angles.

Right triangle
30°
90° 60°
Has one right angle.

Obtuse triangle
30°
110°   40°
Has one obtuse angle.

Youngsters are usually introduced to a variety of other geometrical figures while still in elementary school. The quadrilaterals (four-sided figures) include the parallelogram (two pairs of parallel sides and two pairs of equal sides), the rhombus (a parallelogram with four equal sides), the rectangle (a parallelogram with four right angles), the square (a rectangle with four equal sides), and the trapezoid (which has only one pair of parallel sides):

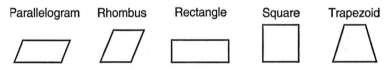

Parallelogram   Rhombus   Rectangle   Square   Trapezoid

Children also usually encounter various other polygons (figures with sides made of line segments). The regular polygons, which have equal sides and equal angles, include the pentagon (five sides), hexagon (six sides), octagon (eight sides), and decagon (ten sides):

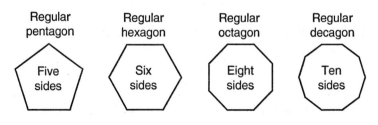

Regular pentagon — Five sides
Regular hexagon — Six sides
Regular octagon — Eight sides
Regular decagon — Ten sides

And, of course, there is the most familiar of all geometrical figures: the circle. Children should know the various measures of circles, such as the chord (line segment that has endpoints on the circle), the diameter (a chord that passes through the center of the circle), the radius (a line segment from the center to any point on the circle), and the tangent (a line that intersects the circle at exactly one point). They should also know how to construct circles of different dimensions using a compass. A compass is an instrument with a point on one end and a pencil on the other end, that is used to make circles by twisting the wrist in a circular motion. To help children learn how to construct and recognize the various geometrical figures, parents should spend some time showing them how to draw these figures.

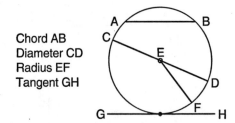

After learning about the various geometrical figures, children usually are taught to compare and manipulate them. For example, they learn that two or more figures are congruent if they have exactly the same shape and size. Children also learn that figures are similar—as opposed to congruent—if they have the same shape but not necessarily the same size:

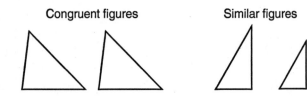

Another important concept is the line of symmetry, which means that if a figure is folded over this line then one half would exactly fit over the other half. The following examples show lines of symmetry for several different geometric figures:

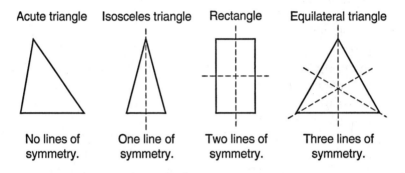

Acute triangle	Isosceles triangle	Rectangle	Equilateral triangle
No lines of symmetry.	One line of symmetry.	Two lines of symmetry.	Three lines of symmetry.

Concepts of manipulation of geometric figures include translation, reflection, and rotation. A figure is translated if you can slide the figure along a straight line. If a figure is reflected, you can flip the entire figure across a line of symmetry. And finally, if a figure is rotated, you can turn it along a curved path around a point. Children need to become familiar with these operations so they can recognize the same figure in different positions:

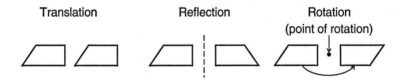

Translation	Reflection	Rotation (point of rotation)

The next thing youngsters learn about geometrical figures are the concepts of perimeter, area, and volume. Perimeter is just the distance around a geometrical figure. For any polygon, the perimeter is the sum of the length of its sides. Formulae are used for common figures, such as: the perimeter (P) of a rectangle is two times its length

(l) plus two times its width (w); the perimeter (P) of a square is just four times the length of one of its sides (s):

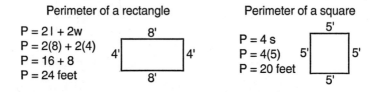

Perimeter of a rectangle

P = 2l + 2w
P = 2(8) + 2(4)
P = 16 + 8
P = 24 feet

Perimeter of a square

P = 4 s
P = 4(5)
P = 20 feet

Finding the circumference of a circle (the length of its perimeter) sometimes poses a little more difficulty for children because the formula involves the "mysterious" concept of π, pronounced "pi." The Greek letter π is merely the ratio of the circumference of a circle to its diameter, and this ratio (approximately equal to 3.14) is the same for any circle. Therefore, the circumference (C) of any circle is just π times its diameter (d), or the more familiar formula of two times π times the radius (r):

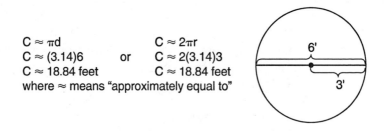

$C \approx \pi d$ $C \approx 2\pi r$
$C \approx (3.14)6$ or $C \approx 2(3.14)3$
$C \approx 18.84$ feet $C \approx 18.84$ feet
where $\approx$ means "approximately equal to"

The concept of area is best explained as the number of square units needed to cover a polygon. This is readily seen with rectangles and squares, which can be filled with square units measuring one unit of length on each side. It is easy to count up the number of square units, and understand why the area (A) of a rectangle is equal to its length (l) times width (w), and why the area (A) of a square is one side (s) times another (do not forget to square the units you are working with):

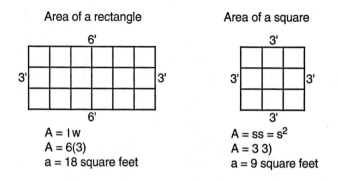

Area of a rectangle

$A = lw$
$A = 6(3)$
$a = 18$ square feet

Area of a square

$A = ss = s^2$
$A = 3\ 3)$
$a = 9$ square feet

Notice the use of the exponent 2 in the formula for the area of a square, when a value is multiplied by itself. I will have more to say on exponents in the upcoming discussion on algebra.

In a similar fashion, it should be easy for children to learn that the area (A) of a parallelogram is equal to its base (b) times height (h). By drawing a line through the parallelogram, thus creating two triangles, it is also easy to see why the area (A) of a triangle is equal to one-half times its base (b) times its height (h). The concept of area for a circle is a little harder for children to understand, but with the familiar formula (area (A) equals π times the radius (r) squared), they should not have too much difficulty computing it:

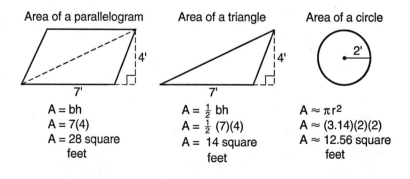

Area of a parallelogram

$A = bh$
$A = 7(4)$
$A = 28$ square feet

Area of a triangle

$A = \frac{1}{2} bh$
$A = \frac{1}{2} (7)(4)$
$A = 14$ square feet

Area of a circle

$A \approx \pi r^2$
$A \approx (3.14)(2)(2)$
$A \approx 12.56$ square feet

When a child learns about solid figures, as a precursor to solid geometry, the concept is both easier and harder to understand. It is easier because the figures can be related to the three-dimensional world in which we live, and it is harder because the formulas and computations are more involved. Youngsters will be introduced to a number of geometrical figures, such as cubes, prisms, pyramids, cones, cylinders, and spheres. When asked to compute the surface areas of these figures, children should think of the figures they are familiar with in two dimensions, and merely extend them along a third dimension. Similarly, when they are asked to understand the concept of volume, they should initially think of how many small cubes (having unitary length, width, and height) will fit into a larger cube. This makes it easier to understand the concept of volume when it is extended to other geometrical figures.

When children take courses in plane and solid geometry, they will be required to learn more complex concepts and solve more difficult problems. The beginning point is knowledge of the various definitions in geometry, so they will understand the concepts presented and be able to express themselves clearly. Since not everything can be proved in a geometric system, they must also be able to understand assumptions or postulates (also called axioms) that are made. Success in geometry will also require some ability in inductive and deductive reasoning, and an understanding of the logical structure of sentences.

Children need to know these things because they will be asked to solve various proofs for geometrical theorems. (A theorem is just a statement or proposition about geometrical relationships.) Proofs involve a formal approach in which statements are presented in logical order, and reasons are given for each statement, in order to prove the theorem. Parents who have helped their children with geometry surely know that solving proofs is usually what presents children with the most difficulty in geometry. Since these proofs often involve the basic geometrical figures and concepts that we have already discussed, it is essential for children to have a solid understanding of this material if they are to succeed with the more difficult concepts.

As an example of the need for mastering basic concepts, children will not be able to understand the Pythagorean Theorem if they do not understand what a right triangle is. Parents can help by working with their children to make sure that they understand the concepts and know how to apply them at each step along the way. Since the Pythagorean Theorem is one of the most important theorems in mathematics, I will state it briefly here. This theorem, which was named after the ancient Greek Pythagoras, allows you to find the length of any side of a right triangle, given the lengths of the other two sides. Before stating this theorem, it is useful to consider the following right triangle:

Side a is called a leg of the triangle.
Side b is also called a leg of the triangle.
Side c is called the hypotenuse of the triangle.

The Pythagorean Theorem states that, for any given right triangle, the square of the length of the hypotenuse equals the sum of the squares of the lengths of the other two legs. Symbolically, we can represent this relationship as:

$$c^2 = a^2 + b^2$$

To illustrate the application of this theorem, we will calculate the length of the hypotenuse for the right triangle shown below:

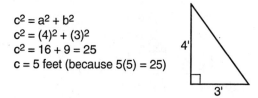

$$c^2 = a^2 + b^2$$
$$c^2 = (4)^2 + (3)^2$$
$$c^2 = 16 + 9 = 25$$
$$c = 5 \text{ feet (because } 5(5) = 25)$$

Children will have frequent occasion to use the Pythagorean Theorem as they advance further in the subject of mathematics. This theorem can be used to find the distance between two points, and in many other applications as well.

Algebra

Algebra is similar to arithmetic in that it deals with the same fundamental operations with numbers—addition, subtraction, multiplication, and division—but it is different in that it uses letters to represent some of the numbers. For example, instead of referring to numbers such as 3, 6, or 8, I might refer to unknown values such as x, y, or z. If children realize that this is the basic distinction, and that algebra builds on much of what they already know, then they will not be intimidated by the subject.

The starting point for algebra is the same as arithmetic, with natural numbers (or counting numbers). Except now, we add negative numbers and zero, and represent them on a number line rather than on fingers. In between the whole numbers are fractional numbers, which can also be represented by a decimal value.

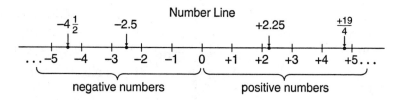

Children should become very comfortable with comparisons between numbers, and understand the distinctions between less than (<), greater than (>), and equal to (=). As we move to the right along the number line, the numbers get larger. And, as we move to the left along the number line, the numbers get smaller. Thus, any number to the right of another number is larger than that number, and any number to the left of another number is smaller than that number. For the numbers shown on the number line above, we can conclude the following:

$$-4\frac{1}{2} < -2.5 \qquad -4\frac{1}{2} < \frac{19}{4} \qquad 2.25 > -2.5 \qquad \frac{19}{4} > 2.25$$

(Notice that it is not necessary to use a + sign for the positive numbers.)

Another important concept for children to master is the absolute value of a number, which is just the distance between the number and zero on the number line, without regard for direction. For example, looking at the number line above, the distance between 0 and 3 is three units, and the distance between 0 and -4 is four units. Thus, the absolute value of a number can never be negative. We represent the absolute value of a number by drawing two vertical lines (| |) around it. Here are some examples:

$$|4| = 4 \qquad |-2| = 2 \qquad |-51| = 51 \qquad |-2.5| = 2.5 \qquad |16| = 16$$

(Note that the absolute value of a number is just the number itself, without its sign.)

The concept of absolute value is important in order to know how to perform arithmetical operations (addition, subtraction, multiplication, and division) with signed numbers (both positive and negative numbers). Here are a few simple rules that you can use to help your child perform these operations:

Addition

To add two numbers with the *same sign*, add their absolute values and assign the same sign to their sum:

$$(+14)+(+7)=+21 \qquad\qquad (-6)+(-8)=-14$$

To add two numbers with *different signs*, subtract the smaller absolute value from the larger one, and assign the sum the same sign as the number with the larger absolute value:

$$(-7)+(+14)=+7 \qquad\qquad (-17)+(+9)=-8$$

Subtraction

To subtract one signed number from another one, change the subtraction symbol to addition and change the sign of the number being subtracted. Then proceed as when adding signed numbers:

$$(+8)-(-3)=(+8)+(+3)=+11 \qquad (-6)-(-2)=(-6)+(+2)=-4$$

Multiplication

To multiply two signed numbers together, first multiply their absolute values together. The product will be positive if the two numbers have the same sign. The product will be negative if the two numbers have different signs:

$$(4)(5)=(20) \qquad (-6)(8)=-48 \qquad (3)(-7)=-21 \qquad (-9)(-9)=81$$

Division

To divide one signed number by another, first divide their absolute values. The quotient is positive if the signed numbers have the same sign, and the quotient is negative if the signed numbers have different signs:

$$(48) \div (6) = 8 \qquad (-35) \div (7) = -5 \qquad (42) \div (-6) = -7 \qquad (-56) \div (-7) = 8$$

In algebra, children are also required to use the various properties of numbers that they learned in arithmetic—the commutative, associative, and distributive properties, as well as the zero and identity properties. These properties are the same as in basic arithmetic, except that letters are used as well as numbers. Learning these properties the first time around makes it much easier to apply them in algebra.

Other important operations with numbers in algebra concern powers and roots. The best way to explain the concept of powers to children is that if a number (say four) is multiplied by itself for a given number of times (say one time), we describe the number as "four to the second power," and write it as four with the number two (the exponent) in its upper right corner. The result of this operation is the number sixteen. We can also ask ourselves what number multiplied by itself equals sixteen, and the result is four. Thus, four is said to be the square root ($\sqrt{}$) of sixteen:

$$(4)(4) = 4^2 = 16 \qquad\qquad \sqrt{16} = 4 \quad \text{because } (4)(4) = 16$$

Youngsters should know how to raise both positive and negative numbers to higher orders, and that they cannot take the square root of a negative number (unless it is what is known as an imaginary number). They must also know the rules of performing various operations with exponents and roots, such as multiplication and division. Understanding how to work with powers and roots is essential, because both are used so frequently in algebra.

So far, we have discussed individual operations in algebra. But most algebraic expressions usually involve multiple operations. For example, a single expression might involve raising some numbers to a power, multiplying or dividing other groups of numbers, and adding or subtracting other numbers. For children to get the right answer, they must understand the proper order of operations.

Here are a few simple rules that parents can use to help their children. If there are any parentheses in an expression, then the operations inside the parentheses must be evaluated before anything else. Then, there are three basic steps in evaluating an expression: first, powers and roots can be performed in any order; second, multiplication and division must be performed in order from left to right; and third, addition and subtraction must also be performed in order from left to right. The following example illustrates these steps:

$$3 \quad (1+5)^2 \quad -4\sqrt{(7+9)} \quad -9 \quad \text{Do the part inside parentheses first.}$$
$$= 3 \quad (6)^2 \quad -4\sqrt{16} \quad -9 \quad \text{Then take powers and roots.}$$
$$= 3 \ (36) \quad -4 \ (4) \quad -9 \quad \text{Then do multiplication from left to right.}$$
$$= 108 \quad -16 \quad -9 \quad \text{Then do subtraction from left to right.}$$
$$= \quad 83 \quad \text{This gives the final answer.}$$

If the operations are performed in any other order, they may result in an incorrect answer. Many problems youngsters encounter in beginning as well as more advanced algebra are due to a lack of understanding of these basic rules.

After children have mastered these operations, they are then prepared to work with algebraic expressions involving letters and symbols. To make this task easier, they should understand certain fundamental definitions. An algebraic expression may contain a variety of numbers, variables, arithmetical operations, and groupings. An example of an algebraic expression is $4 \ x^2 - 3 \ x - 4$. The numbers 4, 2, –3, and –4 are called constants because their value cannot change in this problem. The letter x is called a variable, because its value in the problem can change. We can break this expression into smaller pieces separated by its arithmetic operations. These separate pieces are called terms. By convention, each + or – is considered to be part of the term that follows it. For example, we would identify the terms in this expression as:

$4 x^2$	$-3 x$	-4
First term	Second term	Third term

The numbers and letters being multiplied together in each term are called factors. The part of the term that is a number, such as 4 in the first term, is called the numerical coefficient.

Polynomials are algebraic expressions with terms having coefficients and a variable, or variables, that are raised to a positive exponent that is a whole number. (The above expression is called a polynomial in x.) Children must become familiar with polynomials because they will be required to add, subtract, multiply, and divide them. To do this, they will need to know how to combine like terms and perform various arithmetical operations, including those involving exponents. Parents need to work closely with their children to master these basic operations, because they will be used frequently later on.

Even in a beginning course in algebra, children will be required to solve a number of complex problems. Some of the problems involve solving equations with unknown values. An equation has three parts: the left side, the equal sign, and the right side. For example, consider the following equation:

$$8 x + 4 = 4 x - 12$$

What this equation says is that the quantity on the left side is the same as the quantity on the right side. To solve this equation, we must find the unknown number x, that when substituted into the equation, makes the left side equal the right side. To do this, we need to get the unknown value of x on one side of the equation, and a single number on the other side. In manipulating the numbers and letters to accomplish this, one rule is very important: If we perform the same arithmetic operation to both sides of the equation, the value of the equation stays the same. Here is how to solve the equation:

$8x + 4 = 4x - 12$	This is the original expression.
$-4x \qquad -4x$	Subtract 4 x from both sides of the equation.
$\overline{4x + 4 = \quad -12}$	
$-4 \qquad -4$	Subtract 4 from both sides of ther equation.
$\overline{4x = -16}$	
$\overline{4 \qquad 4}$	Divide both sides of the equation by 4.
$x = -4$	This enables us to solve for x.

By inserting –4 back into the original equation, we can ascertain that this is the correct solution, because each side is equal to the other.

Students will be required to solve many more complicated equations than this, but the approach is similar. They will also be required to solve inequalities, which are statements that two expressions are not equal.

Word problems involving unknown values are often difficult to solve. These problems can take a variety of forms, involving proportions, percents, ratios, distance, time, rates, or variations. What makes these problems so difficult is that even after children know what is being requested, they must be able to change a word expression into an algebraic expression. Parents can help by showing how to set up a word problem. The proper approach involves identifying what is to be solved, breaking the problem into small pieces, changing each piece into an algebraic expression, arranging all of the expressions into an equation, and solving it. Here is an example of how it is done. Suppose that the sum of two unknown numbers is 16, and the second number is eight more than the first number. What are the two numbers?

Let x be the first number, and x + 8 be the second number. Then:

x	+	(x + 8)	= 16, so	2 x + 8	=	16	Combine x.
first number	second number			− 8		− 8	Substract 8.
				2 x	=	8	
The first number x = 4.				2		2	Divide by 2.
The second number (x + 8) = 12.				x	=	4	

And 4 + 12 = 16. (Solution is correct.)

Another operation that often gives children difficulty in algebra is factoring. Factoring is simply the process of finding the factors (or divisors) of an expression. When these factors are multiplied together, the result is the original expression. As part of this process, children must know how to do a variety of things such as: find the greatest common factor in the terms of an expression, group like terms together, factor the difference of two squared numbers, as well as factor expressions having three or more terms. The process must continue until the expression is expressed as the product of prime factors (factors that cannot be reduced any further). Factoring is important because it has many applications, such as solving equations. Here is a very simple example of factoring. Factor the expression $9 x^2 + 6 x$.

We can divide this expression into its prime factors in the following manner:

$$9x^2 + 6x = \underbrace{3 \cdot 3 \cdot x \cdot x} + \underbrace{2 \cdot 3 \cdot x}$$

By inspection, we can see that the factor 3 x is the largest factor that is common to both terms. If we divide each of the terms in the original expression by 3 x, we get the following:

$$\frac{9x^2}{3x} + \frac{6x}{3x} = 3x + 2$$

To factor the expression, we multiply 3 x (the greatest common factor) by 3 x + 2. To check that these are the correct factors, multiply them together to make sure they equal the original expression:

$$(3x)(3x + 2) = 3x \cdot 3x + 3x \cdot 2 = 9x^2 + 6x$$

Working with algebraic fractions also causes much difficulty for children, even though it is basically an extension of what they already know about ordinary fractions. They must know how to reduce fractions to their lowest terms, perform arithmetic operations with them, add unlike fractions, and work with complex fractions (fractions having more than one fraction line).

Fortunately, algebra usually becomes much easier for children when they are asked to graph equations on a rectangular coordinate system having a vertical and horizontal axis. Graphing equations allows youngsters to look at a graph—or picture—of what is going on. One of the simplest tasks is graphing the equation of a straight line, finding intercepts with the axes, and determining the slope or steepness of the line. Gradually the subject becomes more complex as it is broadened to include curved lines, the notions of functions and relations, and systems of equations.

Summary

In this chapter, I have only had space to cover the most basic mathematics topics that students encounter in elementary and junior high school. As noted earlier, I will go into these and other topics in much more detail, along with many examples, in the forthcoming *Math Made Simple*. The present chapter should be viewed as an introduction to the subject.

The range of mathematical subjects that children encounter in elementary and junior high school is important in laying a foundation that will enable them to understand higher mathematics later on. During these early years youngsters not only develop basic abilities in mathematics, but also form attitudes about whether they like the subject. The study of mathematics can either be easy or difficult for children, depending upon how much help they get along the way. Good teachers are essential, but the additional assistance of parents at home is just as important. I realize that this may require extra effort on your part, and brushing up on subjects long forgotten, but the investment is very worthwhile. In today's world, our children are more likely to need knowledge of mathematics to get into a challenging and well-paying field.

Principle 3

To help children master mathematics, parents must provide continual help in explaining concepts and solving problems. Don't leave it all up to the teacher!

SUMMARY

Part 2
Mastering the Three R's

PRINCIPLE 1
To help your children become active readers, show them how to preview a book before reading it, and ask questions that lead to a full understanding of the author's message.

PRINCIPLE 2
To write a good paper, select a topic, think up relevant questions, conduct research, develop an outline, then write and rewrite as necessary. Start early!

PRINCIPLE 3
To help children master mathematics, parents must provide continual help in explaining concepts and solving problems. Don't leave it all up to the teacher!

PART 3

A SYSTEM FOR GETTING GOOD GRADES

Overview of the System

The importance of education has been emphasized since the time of the ancient Greeks, and there are any number of guides available on the market, so how have I been able to come up with a new system of study? In my book, *Getting Straight A's*, I described a system for getting top grades that worked not only for me but, subsequently, for hundreds of thousands of other students. In the present book, I have adapted these proven study methods so they will work for elementary and junior-high-school students. In what follows, you will undoubtedly recognize that many of the ten steps in my system are the same as the good study tips you have heard before. The unique aspect is the way I combine them into an integrated system that shows you exactly what to do to help your child get good grades in school.

If you want to understand something, you have to look for its essence. The essence of my study system is very simple: *When teachers test students on their scholastic abilities, they emphasize material presented and discussed specifically in the classroom.* I have found this principle invariably to be true, regardless of the teacher or the grade level. It is almost like a code of ethics to which teachers subscribe. Most feel it is unfair to test students on material that has not been presented in the classroom because students have not had an opportunity to discuss and ask questions about it. Although some other study guides seem to recognize this basic principle, they do not exploit it in an organized and systematic way.

Why would teachers subscribe to this basic principle? Think of the following. Teachers spend a good part of their lifetime studying the concepts and principles of their particular discipline. During these years of study they have worked and reworked these concepts and principles into a form that—in their mind—captures the essence of the subject. Teachers bring the full range and depth of their knowledge and experience into the classroom. They use their classroom presentations to teach students the techniques and approaches that they have found most useful for understanding a subject. When a teacher describes a subject in class, it is not just one way of teaching the subject but, instead, what the teacher feels is the best way. If children can understand everything presented in class, the teacher will be amazed and pleased that they can master in one year the information that took him or her a lifetime to accumulate. Showing the teacher this mastery will get your child a good grade every time!

At this moment some parents probably think that my basic premise is flawed, since they would argue that their children have been tested on material not covered in class or homework assignments that were never discussed. This happens rarely. Teachers normally give homework assignments that provide additional practice on material covered in class. When they plan to test students on material not covered in class, they usually give an advance notice of their intention. The more likely occurrence is that the teacher presented or discussed the material in the classroom but the student failed to hear it. Scientific studies have shown that people are not very good listeners; they retain only a small fraction of the material presented to them.

I can remember many occasions, when I was in school, thinking that the teacher was testing us on material covered outside of the classroom. But upon careful reexamination of my notes or discussion with other students, I discovered that the teacher had indeed presented the material.

I will now show you a simple integrated system that will enable your child to digest and master almost all of the material presented in class. My system covers everything from planning a course of study to making top grades in all of these courses. I have used these methods on different types of courses, and have seen them work for all kinds of students. I have now adapted them so they apply to younger students. Here is my system in ten easy-to-follow-steps.

1

Planning a Course of Study

Plato, the ancient Greek philosopher, said "The direction in which education starts a man will determine his future life." It is important for students to get direction by planning a course of study, so they will have a desirable future life.

Many people go all of the way through school without having any idea of what they want to do for a living. By the time they arrive in college, many students have yet to select their major field of study and end up changing their minds several times over. Even after obtaining a college degree, many entrants into the labor market change jobs several times because they still do not know what they want to do for a living. This ambivalence can prove costly beyond some point because different fields have different requirements and frequent changes of job give the impression that the person is unstable. While most children will take the same types of courses while they are in elementary and junior high school, it is not too early even at this young age to help them decide what profession they would eventually like to choose. Knowing what you want to become is a great motivator because all of the hard work and extra effort in school seems more purposeful.

There are several things parents can discuss with their children to get them pointed in the right direction. In thinking about a future occupation, the most desirable jobs are those that are enjoyable and also pay well. How much you earn is a common denominator, but what we enjoy differs significantly from person to person. If your child is interested in a particular occupation, you should emphasize that education is an important requirement in gaining entry into many fields. Impress upon youngsters that having a college degree has become a necessity for many occupations, and if they want to gain entry into a professional field even more education will be required. Point out that, for example, to become a doctor or lawyer one has to attend many years of medical or law school. Also make it clear one has to have good grades to get into a good college or professional school. Tell children that while a lot of effort is required to enter a worthwhile field, the future will hold many rewards after they have finished. Giving children an objective, and pointing out the rewards, is a good way to help focus.

It is difficult for youngsters to appreciate the requirements of different types of jobs, because they have not worked. As they get older, many will get experience by working during the summer, but rarely will these summer jobs offer the complexity and problems faced in a profession. For this reason, parents need to describe to their children what is required in different lines of work. As a starting point, you can talk about your own occupation and what you must do during a typical work day.

Additional perspectives can be gained by talking to other adults in different lines of work. When going on family outings, parents should describe the occupations of people they see at work, what is required to get into them, what the work involves, and roughly how much these jobs pay. You should also take children to a factory where they can see the activities of workers and gain a better appreciation of how things are made. Many factories offer free tours as a way of promoting better public relations.

A number of government publications contain information about different occupations. The U.S. Bureau of the Census, where I work, produces several reports showing the earnings levels and personal characteristics of workers employed in various jobs. The U.S. Bureau of Labor Statistics publishes estimates on the number of workers who will be employed in different occupations. One of their publications that is particularly useful for job planning is the *Occupational Outlook Handbook*, which is updated regularly. This handbook contains valuable information on training requirements, working conditions, and employment opportunities for about 225 different occupations, which comprise about 80 percent of all jobs in the economy. These reports should be available in your local library. They contain very important information for planning a career, and should be of use to your child in thinking about a future job.

Even during a child's early years, schools offer assistance to students on career planning. In elementary school, teachers often give special assignments on the kinds of activities associated with different occupations. By the time children reach junior high school, counselors work with them on selecting a course of study for entering college, and often discuss career planning. In college, there are counseling centers that provide information on the characteristics of different jobs as well as job availabilities. Sometimes colleges sponsor job fairs, which are attended by representatives from companies looking for entry-level workers. In all of these activities, parents should help their children make informed decisions about career planning.

In working with their children, parents should help them make a realistic assessment of their capabilities and limitations as a student. Parents should be candid about fields that have given them difficulty in the past and about weaknesses in basic skills. If parents feel that their children lack proficiency in the basic skills—such as reading, comprehension, or writing—then they should encourage them to take a special course in a reading and study skills laboratory. These laboratories often provide teaching machines that give students practice at reading faster and test their comprehension through a series of questions and answers. They also have programmed texts designed to broaden students' vocabulary, increase their comprehension, and improve their study skills. It is silly not to take advantage of these services if they are available, even if your child is an above-average student.

Soon after children enter school, they are often assigned an adviser who helps them plan a course of study. Normally this is done in conjunction with the parents' assistance, and parents have to approve their children's courses. Most schools require students to take a certain number of courses in basic fields such as English, social studies, mathematics, and the sciences. If you want your youngster to receive a solid education and prepare adequately for college, it is important that your child enters an academic track. Some schools also have a more general or technical track, but children in this track often do not receive the rigorous preparation they will need for college. Although the tracking of students is discouraged and even illegal in some areas, schools seem to have an uncanny ability to group the brighter students together in classes where they can learn at a more rapid rate. Some school systems have special programs and even special schools for gifted and talented students. It is important for parents to get their children into the right environment where they will be challenged and encouraged to learn as much as they can. It may mean more work for the student, but it will pay big dividends in the long run.

If your child has the option of taking electives, then I strongly recommend courses in writing, art, music, and drama. As I mentioned earlier, most people lack basic writing skills. An elective in expository or creative writing will help develop those skills, which can then be used in other subjects, since writing of some kind is required in most courses. Art teaches an appreciation of our physical environment, develops an ability to represent it through drawings and paintings, and provides a fascinating history of visual creativity. Music not only satisfies the musically inclined, but also helps develop discipline in all of us. And drama teaches us how to express ourselves verbally, a skill that can be transferred to many other subjects.

In helping your child to plan a course of study, it is important that he or she takes courses in the proper order. Every subject has a natural progression from relatively easy to more difficult levels of learning. Many higher-level courses require a knowledge of material presented at lower levels. Building a house is a fitting analogy. You need a good foundation before you can erect the walls. By taking the lower-level courses first, children develop a solid foundation, and the higher-level courses will be easier when they eventually take them. Most courses either have specific prerequisites or are only offered in specific grades. If there is any question, you should check first with your child's counselor or teacher about the proper level of preparation. When youngsters take courses out of sequence, they only make things unnecessarily difficult for themselves.

If your child experiences serious difficulty with a class, there are several things you can do. As a first step, you might ask for assistance from a tutor at school. If the material seems too complicated, you should encourage your youngster to attend a more appropriate course. Sometimes students find themselves in trouble when they have transferred from another school with less demanding standards. Precocious students who have skipped a grade also occasionally find themselves in trouble if they have missed some basic material. Parents and their children should confront such problems directly rather than ignore them, so they do not become more serious later on.

In planning a course of study for your child, I advise you to avoid televised classes if possible. Some schools use TV to make an outstanding teacher available to all students. Moreover, teaching with television insures the same basic material needed to master a subject is presented to all students. Some recent technology even allows youngsters to ask questions of the teacher on the television set. In my opinion, elementary and junior-high-school students can easily be distracted in televised classes. The experience is too similar to watching their favorite television programs at home. Rather than the passive experience of viewing TV, I believe it is more productive to enroll students in courses where they can obtain individual attention from a teacher present in the classroom.

Once you have planned a course of study for children, talk to them frequently about what they want to accomplish. Explain that success does not come overnight, and that all of us have to travel a long way to reach our goals and objectives, but tell them that they are on the right track for getting into college. If they occasionally experience difficulty with some courses, encourage them to tough it out and emphasize that exposure to a wide range of material is needed to become educated. Give a child some leeway in taking some of the electives that he or she is interested in. Above all else, make your youngsters feel that they are on an important mission, and that they can reach their goals by following the course of study that has been laid out for them.

Principle 1
Plan a course of study for children, and work hard to keep them on the right track.

2
Working with Teachers

Over two thousand years ago the Latin philosopher Cicero said, "What greater or better gift can we offer the republic than to teach and instruct our youth?" Teachers are involved in an important mission, both to our families and our nation. In order to help teachers do their job, we must work closely with them.

To begin we must recognize that teaching is a difficult job. We often hear people say that teaching is easy, because teachers work less than eight hours each day, earn pretty good pay, and get time off for holidays and the long summer vacation. What they don't say is that teachers put in many more hours than the time spent in the classroom, preparing for classes and grading examinations.

It is also important to realize that most people are in their profession because they love to teach. Considering their high level of educational attainment, they could probably find a much better-paying job in the private sector. But most of them teach because they enjoy the intellectual challenge and the opportunity to impart knowledge. There is nothing that gives teachers more pleasure than to see their students master a difficult subject and grow intellectually. They know that they play an important role in developing the great leaders and thinkers of the future. Since a teacher has your child's interest at heart, it should be clear that he or she is your friend rather than your foe in the learning process.

Unlike college students, who can select their professors, younger students are assigned teachers by their schools. Elementary-school pupils often have one teacher for all or most of their subjects, while junior-high-school students are assigned a different teacher for each subject. The quality of teachers naturally varies—so how do you know if your child has a good one? The best teachers are knowledgeable about their subject, cover a large volume of substantive material in the classroom, treat students in a fair-minded manner, and are good communicators. In addition, a really good teacher is dedicated and persistent in developing not just the brightest students, but also the slower learners.

Obviously, it is hard to find a teacher who scores at the top on *all* counts; most are stronger in some areas than others. And do not fall into the trap of thinking that the easiest teacher is the best teacher, because even though children may get good grades under such circumstances, they must also eventually deal with more difficult teachers when the subject becomes more complex and harder to learn. There is seldom much that parents can do about selecting teachers, unless the teacher is a real failure. Requesting a change in instructors can create the impression among school administrators that yours is a problem child. It is far better to work with the teacher and help compensate for any shortcomings.

There are several things that parents can do to get better acquainted with their children's teachers. Many schools offer an orientation program for parents, especially when students are first entering either elementary school or junior high school. During these sessions, parents are introduced to the various facilities, administrators, teachers, and programs in the school. Some schools even provide orientation programs for parents of students returning to the school the following year. These sessions are particularly useful because they offer parents the opportunity to meet their children's teachers before or soon after school begins. Time is usually allotted for teachers to explain to parents what subjects will be covered during the year, what is expected in the way of assignments, and how children will be graded. This gives parents an idea of whether or not it corroborates the information their children will bring home from school. Meeting personally with teachers during these informal gatherings also offers parents an opportunity to mention any special characteristics or interests their children may possess.

During orientation, the Parents and Teachers Association (PTA) often looks for willing parents to help out with various activities at school. The activities may include helping organize school-related functions, providing assistance as a teacher's aide, or accompanying the class on field trips. All of these occasions provide an opportunity to get to know teachers better. Sometimes teachers ask parents with special skills to make a presentation to the class on a subject of interest. On many occasions I have given talks to students on how they can improve their study habits and raise their grades in school. Administrators and teachers appreciate the assistance of parents because they are often short on help, and the presence of parents helps to establish their role as partners in the learning process. You should try to participate in as many of these activities as possible.

Most teachers schedule a set number of conferences during the year, to meet with parents and discuss their children's progress. During these sessions teachers give parents a candid assessment of their children's progress and identify problem areas. This gives teachers the

opportunity to discuss the specifics of classroom performance, and to make recommendations on what parents
can do at home to remedy weaknesses or reinforce
strengths. It also provides parents with the opportunity to
discuss their children's study habits as well as anything
else that concerns them. In order to make progress, it is
essential for parents and teachers to be absolutely candid
so they can work together to overcome problems. Parents
should take the teacher's recommendations very seriously, and make extra efforts with their children in
appropriate areas. A saving grace is that conferences are
often held before the grading period so there is still time
to do something before the report card comes home.

Another way that parents can work with teachers is to
find out how they can compensate for missed material.
There are times when children cannot be in school
because of illness or family vacations—although parents
should try, if at all possible, to avoid making their youngsters miss school. If classes must be missed, parents
should visit the teacher and obtain reading materials or
other assignments that children can work on while away.
It is important for parents to make sure that their youngsters actually do their assignments, and to provide additional assistance as the teacher would in the classroom.
Doing this keeps children from falling behind in their
studies. Moreover, teachers are impressed by parents who
care about their offspring and are willing to assume an
active role in the learning process.

Parents should always remember that they and their
children's teachers are partners in the learning process.
By working together they can jointly accomplish their
goals. If they are at odds the result can be a frustrated and
confused child. For this reason, parents should try to
avoid confrontations or arguments with their children's
teachers. If you have a disagreement with a teacher, try to

resolve the problem in a calm and civilized manner. Do not go over the teacher's head and complain to a principal or administrator unless you are faced with a situation that absolutely demands it. Identify areas of agreement and seek to resolve areas of disagreement. If you work well with teachers, the learning process will be easier and more productive for you, your child, and the teacher. Remember . . .

Principle 2
You must work effectively with teachers for your child to succeed in school.

3
Attending Class Regularly

"Miss not the discourse of the elders," advises the Old Testament Book of Ecclesiastes. What was wise thousands of years ago remains wise today. Your child should attend every class in school, because the elders—the teachers—will probably discuss important material, and it may show up on a test.

Children should be allowed to miss classes only when they have a legitimate excuse. There are plenty of times when children want to stay home merely because they do not feel like going to school. All parents have had experiences with children who do not want to get out of bed in the morning because they stayed up too late the night before and are tired. Others may want to remain home because they have not done their homework, or seek to avoid some specific activity at school that day. Still others find school boring, and wish to do something else such as play video games. Needless to say, none of these are legitimate excuses. The only real excuse for children to miss school is that they are too ill to attend. Too ill does not mean a slight headache or a runny nose, it means an illness that is contagious or severe enough to prevent a child from functioning properly in school. When children are this sick, parents should take them to see a doctor.

Students should realize that they run a risk when they miss a class, because examinations may include questions on material covered while they were absent. If an exam only has three or four essay questions and the student misses one of them, then the best grade he or she can receive might be only a C. Sometimes an entire question is drawn from a single lecture, and the answer cannot be found in any of the reading materials. A student absent that day will be at a disadvantage, even if he has considerable knowledge of the rest of the material.

When I say that students should never miss a class, that includes not missing even part of that day's instruction. Students should always try to get to class on time, even if this means they must get out of bed earlier than they wish. Parents can help by making sure their children get on a good schedule.

Many teachers often use the first five minutes to summarize what they covered previously or to make assignments for future classes. And by all means, tell youngsters not to pack their belongings five minutes before the class is over so they can make a mad rush for the door as soon as the bell rings. Such behavior is viewed as bad manners, and gives the impression that the student is not really interested in the subject. Although it may not seem fair, the impressions that children create can influence the grades they receive, particularly if they do borderline work.

It is useful to tell children that even if their teachers base their lectures entirely on the reading material, they will miss something significant by not attending class. Attending classroom lectures changes people in certain ways. The teacher will introduce new ideas to children. It is likely that students will leave the classroom with a different view of the world than when they entered. Learning continues for children outside the classroom, even during times when they are not studying. Their minds will probably be reviewing and synthesizing this new material at various times during the day, even when they are involved in everyday activities. This learning process may take place while children are getting dressed, eating, walking to class, participating in recreation with their friends, or in a number of other situations. You may find your child silently reciting new facts or working over new problems that the teacher presented in class. If children do not attend class, there is no opportunity for this type of learning to take place.

The worst possible time for children to miss class is toward the end of the school year. Ironically, many students do so during this period because the days are pleasant and inviting. The final classes of the semester are often used to review and outline the entire course, or to mention what topics will be part of the final exam. Some teachers even go so far as to tell students what questions will be on the final test or at least the possible range of questions. Other teachers use the last class as a general question-and-answer period for everyone, and some of these questions may actually show up on the exam. When children miss the last few classes, they are at a significant disadvantage in competing against their classmates.

If children absolutely cannot attend a class, then parents should meet with the teacher to find out what was missed. It may be possible to get materials covered in class, or at least find out about homework assignments in textbooks. Unless children are too ill to study, parents should bring these materials home and see that their youngsters keep up with the work. Even mildly ill children often do not feel like doing homework, so parents may have to persuade them to make an extra effort. It is important for children to hand in completed work when they return to school, so the teacher will know that they kept up with their studies while they were absent. Doing this creates a very good impression on the teacher.

It is often said that the best way to teach children is by example. Well, here is an example that they can use as a goal. During my entire graduate curriculum, when I was working for my Ph.D., I never missed or was late for one class. There were plenty of times when I could have been doing something else, but I always resisted the temptation. I can even remember going to class with a severe case of the flu and a 104-degree fever. Now I look back and realize that this was an extreme thing to do, but at the time I was concerned that the teacher might present material that would appear later on a test. I am not recommending that children do the same but, by the same token, they should not miss class indiscriminately. As the old saying goes, "You will be surprised at what you can do, if you feel that you have to do it!"

Principle 3
Don't allow children to miss class unless they are genuinely too ill to attend.

4

Sitting in the Best Spot

The American poet Emily Dickinson once wrote, "But, looking back—the first so seems to comprehend the whole." Children are much more likely to "comprehend the whole" of what the teacher is saying when they sit in the front row. This is unquestionably the best place for youngsters to be in the classroom. They will absorb much more of the material in the front row because they are more likely to remain oblivious to everything else going on around them. They can see only the teacher and the blackboard, and they will be able to absorb the nuance of every word and thought.

When children sit in the front row, the teacher knows that they are there to learn. The teacher is more likely to recognize students in the front row and think of them as individuals, rather than a name or number on a sheet of paper. This is important because, with limited resources, classes in some schools have become quite large. It is more difficult for children to get individual attention in a large class, but those in the front row are more likely to interact with the teacher.

If given a choice of where to sit, most children—and most adults—will gravitate toward the middle or back of the classroom. People do not like to sit in the first row because they feel more vulnerable. Youngsters know that not only will they have less privacy in the front row, the teacher is more likely to call on them to answer a question. Some may fear that as a result they will reveal their ignorance about a subject, embarrassing themselves in front of their classmates. They must be attentive and prepared when they sit in the front row, and that is precisely why they should go there. Children will get more out of their teacher's lectures if they are awake and alert rather than in a daydream.

There is a saying that, "Time flies when you are having fun!" The phrase is usually used disparagingly to describe how slowly time seems to pass when you are bored. I remember becoming so absorbed in what the teacher was saying that, by the time the lecture was over, I felt as if I had just walked into the classroom. It was the same feeling one sometimes gets when participating in a favorite sport or activity. When children start to feel this way in the classroom, the whole learning experience becomes more enjoyable.

I realize in a class of thirty or so students, not everyone can sit in the front row. In some classes the teacher offers seating on a first-come, first-served basis. In other classes the teacher assigns seating, possibly with some rotation during the year. If seating is open, encourage your child to get there early and sit up front. If seating is assigned, you may want to request that your child be given a front-row seat. If your child has a hearing or vision limitation this is always a good justification, but so is your judgment that your child will learn more up front. If your child cannot get a front row seat, encourage her to sit as close to the front as possible and not worry about it. Many teachers who are learning the importance of this basic principle now move through the class so all students feel as though they are up front at some time during the class.

But sitting elsewhere is never quite the same because the teacher returns to the front of the room periodically to write on the blackboard.

Sitting in the front row may seem like a small thing, but it is one of the most important steps in my system of study. If you want your child to "comprehend the whole" of what the teacher has to say, then follow—

Principle 4
Make sure that children sit in
the front row of the class.

5

Completing Assignments on Time

Louis Pasteur, the French chemist who invented pasteurization, said, "In the fields of observation, chance favors only the mind that is prepared." What applies to scientific observation also holds true for the classroom. If children are to be prepared for their next class, they must complete their homework assignments beforehand.

Homework that teachers give typically falls into two categories: written assignments and reading assignments. Written assignments provide the teacher with immediate information about how much work students have done and how well they have understood it. Although reading assignments do not provide this kind of immediate feedback to the teacher, they are every bit as important for understanding the subject. Reading assignments will determine how much children learn from their teachers' lectures and, ultimately, how well they do in the subject.

The first task is for you and your child to find out what will be expected in the way of homework assignments. As I noted earlier, during school orientation many teachers describe to parents what they expect to cover during the coming year, and what is expected for homework assignments. Some teachers also hand out a course outline at the beginning of the year. The outline tells youngsters what material will be covered in the course over the duration of the term or year, what will be expected in the way of homework assignments, and also when assignments are due. In fact, some better-organized teachers even hand out an outline listing the reading and written homework assignments for each class, or each week. If your child's teacher has not provided an outline or reading schedule, you should try to make one up. Encourage your child to ask the teacher at the end of each class about the material to be read for the next or future classes. If you are not getting anywhere with this approach, do not hesitate to call your child's teacher and ask for the information yourself. Some of the better teachers also supply parents with their telephone numbers, and encourage them to call when necessary.

Most teachers include in their outlines a list of the books your child is expected to read during the term or year. In elementary and junior high school, textbooks are usually provided free of charge to the student. Schools and teachers select particular textbooks because they think that these books have an advantage over other books on the market either in content or method of presentation. In all likelihood, the textbooks selected will serve as a useful introduction to the subjects to be studied and will complement the material covered by teachers during their lectures. Teachers also include in their outlines supplementary or recommended books for book reports and other assignments. If you decide not to purchase these books, you should make provision to obtain them either from the library or other sources. It is important for children to have ready access to all of the books needed for their work.

The most important advice about textbooks and other assigned books is that children must read them. It will not do any good if these books sit around gathering dust. When should children read their assignments? Usually before the next class in which the subject will be discussed. That is the most important advice given in this chapter.

Completing reading assignments before class familiarizes children with the material and makes it easier for them to comprehend and retain when the teacher presents it in class. When children schedule their reading in this manner, they will find their teachers' lectures to be more interesting and exciting, and they will be better able to organize and digest the material presented to them. They will also become more active listeners because they already know something about the subject. It is easier for the mind to process information the second time around, because it has already resolved many of the problems and questions encountered initially.

If children do not understand something about the subject after their first reading of the material, then they should ask for clarification in the classroom. They can bring up their queries with their teacher before, during, or after the class, whichever is most appropriate. Children should not be shy or afraid that the teacher or their classmates will think they are ignorant for asking a silly question. Tell your children that if they have a question, they should raise it; if they have nothing to say, they should remain silent. If children have done their reading assignments ahead of time, they should be able to answer many of the questions raised in class by the teacher. This will show the teacher that they are mentally sharp and well-prepared.

It is important for children to understand that reading assignments are a means to an end, and not an end in itself. If they do not fully understand a reading assignment the first time, then they should read it again. Parents should emphasize to children that they should try to complete the reading *before* they attend the class in which the material will be discussed. Discourage children from going back and reading the material after class, because they will only find themselves falling behind. There are exceptions: sometimes a teacher tells the class to review specific portions of the reading assignments because they will be covered on a test.

During my many years of schooling, I have seen some students make an absolute fetish out of the reading assignments. They underline extensive passages in their books, using various shades of pen and magic marker, and they read and reread the passages several times in preparation for a test. Students most likely to use this approach do not attend class regularly or take only few notes when they do attend. Although this approach may appear to make sense, it is really a waste of time. Most teachers do not care how much of the reading material their students can memorize by rote but, rather, how well they have understood the concepts presented in class. Also parents may have to pay for marked-up books, because students in elementary and junior high school normally have to return textbooks at the end of the year.

Parents should give their children some additional advice about looking for shortcuts around reading assignments. Tell them they should not assume they can ignore reading assignments because they think the teacher will cover all of the material in class that will appear later on exam questions. Emphasize that they need to do the readings to obtain a complete grasp of the subject the teacher presents in class. Besides, there is a lot more to every subject in school than what the teacher discusses. Since time is limited, teachers sometimes can cover only the most significant aspects of the subject. Supplementary readings usually expand on material discussed in class, and can further stimulate a child's interest. An important lesson that children need to learn about school (and life) comes from an old Italian proverb: "The longest way round is the shortest way home."

Elementary and junior-high-school teachers usually give some form of written homework assignments just about every night. There is a strong and proven belief that children will progress much faster if they practice and refine at night what they have learned in class each day. Thus, children get homework assignments in just about all subjects, including English, social studies, science, and mathematics. In fact, written homework assignments tend to be more frequent and extensive in science and mathematics. This is in the nature of these disciplines, since students master the material by working out real problems, and they cannot go forward until they have mastered the previous step. Simply watching the teacher do math and science problems in class will not teach children all of the nuances of problem solving. They have to roll up their sleeves, and make some mistakes, to really learn the material. Parents should tell their children that the objective is to make the mistakes and learn the proper methods before the teacher gives an exam.

Most teachers in elementary and junior high school are conscientious about collecting homework assignments, grading them, and returning them to the student. It is imperative that children complete these assignments on time, both to send the proper signal to the teacher and to progress at the proper pace. If children do not complete their homework assignments on schedule, they will soon find themselves falling behind—but it is always wise to turn in the homework at some point; even if it is late, there is at least a chance to receive partial credit.

Parents should also tell their children not to think of homework assignments as punishment given out by the teacher but, rather, as a device for helping them become more knowledgeable about a subject. Tell children to approach their homework assignments in earnest and with enthusiasm. If they do so and still do not understand some of their homework questions, then they should seek assistance either from parents or the teacher. It is quite possible that exam questions may be similar to those given as homework.

If parents want to help their children get the most from the teacher's classroom presentations, then they must follow—

Principle 5
Make sure that children complete all homework assignments before attending class.

6
Learning to Take Notes Properly

William Shakespeare once wrote, "It is the disease of not listening, the malady of not marking, that I am troubled withal." What was troubling to Shakespeare remains a problem today. Students must listen carefully to their teacher and take extensive notes in class if they have any hope of becoming straight-A students.

Listening and taking good notes is probably the most crucial part of my entire system. Children should make an effort to capture everything of importance that the teacher presents, because they will be tested largely on material covered during class lectures. To capture everything they will need to use all of their listening ability and concentration during class, and to have a good system for recording what the teacher says. These tasks are a big demand for small children, who often have difficulty concentrating for long periods of time, but it is essential for their success in school. If they obtain little or nothing from their classroom lectures, the whole learning experience will prove more difficult. The purpose of this chapter is to show parents how to help their children become more effective listeners and note-takers.

Children may suffer from a number of barriers to effective listening, such as not being interested in the subject, dislike of the teacher, being easily distracted by noise in the classroom or the mannerisms of other children, and lack of concentration. If they hope to become effective listeners, children must work hard to overcome these barriers.

The stage is already set for children to become good listeners if they are sitting in the front row and have read their assignments beforehand, but much more is required. They usually have to learn how to become good listeners on their own—with the help of their parents, of course—because the average school curriculum does not contain courses that teach this skill.

It is important for children to understand that unlike reading, writing, and thinking—over which they have complete control—listening involves the presence of another person. In order to be good listeners, children have to be good followers. They need to focus their concentration on the teacher's line of thought and avoid drifting off on tangents. This is more difficult than it sounds because even children can think several times faster than their teachers can speak. They should use this extra time to think about what their teacher has said, record these statements in their notes, and try to anticipate the teacher's next thought. Tell them that if the teacher says something they find very intriguing, they should avoid thinking about it deeply at that time. There is always plenty of time after class to think deep thoughts. The best strategy is for children to accept temporarily what the teacher says, and be good followers.

Parents should tell their children not to blindly accept everything that the teacher says. Even though they may be experts in their field, teachers do not know everything and occasionally make mistakes. If the teacher says something that youngsters do not understand, tell them to question it. But encourage them to be intelligent about asking questions in class. They should ask a question of the teacher if they really need assistance, but should not be so impatient that they interrupt the teacher or disrupt the class. The main point is that children should ask questions that are worthy of consideration rather than raising questions merely because they wish to be heard. Parents can be helpful by giving children examples of both kinds of questions.

It is important to emphasize to children that good listeners are attentive during class, because they know that they have only one chance to grasp the material. In contrast, they can read a passage in a book several times until they understand it. If children lose their concentration for just a few minutes in class, they run the risk of missing something important that may appear later on a test. In teaching children how to be attentive, encourage them to use all of their senses to gather information during class. Their eyes should alternate between the blackboard and the paper they are writing on, their ears should be keenly attuned to the teacher's words, and their minds should be working on understanding and synthesizing the teacher's thoughts. Their entire being should be involved in understanding the nuance of everything the teacher says.

One of the most effective ways for children to become good listeners is to take good notes. And, by the same token, one of the best ways to take good notes is to be a good listener. Far too often, children in elementary and junior high school take no notes at all. This presents a big problem for them when they get into high school and especially college, because good note-taking is essential for doing well. The key to being a good student later on is to acquire the right habits from the start.

One of the basic needs for taking good notes is proper supplies. While I normally recommend that college students use spiral notebooks with pages that do not come out, I think it is best for elementary and junior-high-school students to use loose-leaf notebooks with pages that can be easily removed. For one thing, children will probably not take as many notes as college students, and teachers are more likely to ask younger students to hand in their work. As with college students, I encourage children to take their notes in pencil and have a good eraser handy. Children are likely to make mistakes when writing, and sometimes teachers make mistakes, too. When children use ink, it is difficult to correct mistakes, and the result is often a messy page that is hard to read. Also make sure that children take to class all of the supplies they will need there, such as rulers, compasses, protractors, and so forth.

I realize that younger children cannot write as fast as older students, but they should nonetheless attempt to copy all the significant thoughts that the teacher expresses in class. Tell children to forget about trying to record the informal discussion, such as jokes and other trivial matters. They should concentrate on recording what the teacher says rather than trying to translate it into their own words. Otherwise, children may become so preoccupied that they miss an important thought, or use words that express a thought incorrectly. I also do not recommend that children try to construct elaborate outlines during class to organize material unless, of course, the teacher has presented one as part of the discussion. On the other hand, if the teacher draws graphs, charts, or tables on the blackboard during class, tell children to be sure to record this information in their notes. The usefulness of your child's notes for studying for an exam is only as good as the information that goes into them.

One way children can capture most of what the teacher says is by using standard abbreviations. They can later translate them into more complete English. For example, children can use the following abbreviations for some standard words and phrases, such as: e.g. (for example), = (equals), ≠ (does not equal), &° (and), w/ (with), w/o (without), and so on. It is important for children to use the same standard abbreviations each time, so they can decipher the word(s) accurately at a later time.

Children should also realize that they do not have to write complete sentences in their notes. They can leave out conjunctions, prepositions, and other words that are not essential to the thought. Young children have to be careful with this approach, however, because they are still learning the fundamentals of the English language and may leave out words that change the meaning of the thought. Their objective should be to write as little as possible, and still capture all of the facts, principles, and ideas expressed by the teacher.

Children need a good system to organize all these notes. Since they are recording their notes in a looseleaf notebook, it is especially important for them to write down the date and page number at the top of each page so they can keep track of what they are doing. They should also make notes about their assignments, what they involve, and when they are due. This makes it much easier for parents and children to sort out what was covered in class each day, and what needs to be done for homework each night.

One of the most challenging tasks is to teach children how to be on the alert for potential exam questions while they are taking their notes. Tell them to look for changes in their teachers' gestures or tone of voice when they are emphasizing a significant principle or idea. When teachers become excited about a subject, there is a good chance that it will show up on an exam. Some become so enthusiastic they are unable to conceal their emotions, and clearly telegraph their intentions. Other teachers are more outspoken, and may even reveal in class that certain subjects will show up on an exam. Being able to spot a potential exam question puts children one step ahead of other students, because they have time to collect their thoughts and prepare an answer beforehand.

Another challenging task is to help children recognize their teacher's style for presenting material in class. Some provide an outline at the beginning of class, others number their main points and repeat them several times for emphasis, while still others hand out written summaries of what they discuss each day. Being able to recognize the teacher's style helps children organize material more effectively and absorb more information because they know what to expect.

I realize younger children may find it difficult to listen and digest material more carefully than they have done before. They will have to work harder in class, but they will learn a lot more. The task will be easier if children start taking notes regularly by the time they are in the third or fourth grade. If children take extensive notes as I have outlined in this section, they will become more involved in the learning process. Their bodies and minds will be working almost every second while they are in class, digesting and synthesizing the material. When children become that involved, they will find time passes quickly, and they are less aware of the amount of work they are doing. Eventually they will feel exhilarated as they gain command over their studies. They will enjoy being a few steps ahead of their classmates, and there is less chance they will be distracted by them. Most important, they will learn valuable skills that will be helpful later on.

I have one more important piece of advice that you can communicate to your children. Tell them not to look for an easy way out of hard work. For example, I do not recommend the use of tape recorders for children in elementary and junior high school, unless they have a very serious problem understanding the teacher. I know that older students sometimes use tape recorders in class, but younger students will probably be less willing to listen to their teacher if they know that a tape recorder is running, which means they can listen later. Besides, it is difficult for children to make much sense out of a tape recording if the teacher refers to something on a blackboard that is no longer in front of them. I firmly believe that children will understand and retain material much better if they write it down shortly after they hear it.

Even if children can fully understand a teacher's lecture without taking notes, this does not absolve them of the need to write down what they are learning. There is no guarantee that children will remember what the teacher said at a later date. The only way for them—and you—to be certain is if they take careful detailed notes.

Principle 6
Encourage your child to take extensive notes during class.

7

Mastering What was Presented
in Class

Euripides, the ancient Greek dramatist, said, "In this world second thoughts, it seems, are best." What was true in ancient times is still true today. Children should always review their school materials a second time, *before* the next class. This includes both the notes they made and their written homework.

I usually recommend that college students rewrite their lecture notes entirely before the next class, but I feel that this approach is not necessary for elementary and junior-high-school students. In most college classes, the student only sees the teacher for a few hours a week, and in many classes there is little opportunity for feedback before a big test. Younger students typically see the same teacher each day—and sometimes for several hours each day—and have ample homework assignments to develop their skills and measure their progress. These students would probably not have time to do all their homework if they spent a large amount of time rewriting their notes. The notes made in class are still important for tests, however, and that is why younger students should make a determined effort to understand them on a continuous basis.

When children come home from school, they should pick a quiet place where they can really concentrate on what they have written in class that day. Although they will not be rewriting their notes, they certainly will be adding to them. This involves translating their abbreviated notes into complete thoughts and sentences, by *neatly* adding words to what they wrote earlier. When children do this, they are resolving any inconsistencies raised during their teachers' lectures. In the process, they should also make sure that they can distinguish major points from minor details.

It may be helpful for children to organize their notes in outline form, but this probably will require some help from parents—especially for younger students. I am not suggesting that children rearrange what the teacher said, only that they add some headings and outline the framework of the discussion. This not only serves as an aid for understanding the material, but develops some valuable skills in outlining as well. Children may want to write personal comments into their notes but, if they do, it is important that they make it clear that these comments are their own rather than the teacher's.

When youngsters review and add to their notes, they should make sure that they really understand what they have written. This means they should review their notes in an active fashion, inquiring about the context and importance of their teachers' statements and, in particular, their relevance for potential exam questions. If children's notes contain inconsistencies that they cannot resolve on their own, then they should ask their parents for assistance. If this still does not solve the problem, then they can raise a question the next day in class or see the teacher. This type of feedback not only ensures that teachers and students are on the same wavelength, it sends an important signal to the teacher that your child is a serious student who is actively engaged in the learning process.

The big advantage of children reviewing their own notes before the next class is that they are forced to rethink the material in a very deliberate way. By adding helpful comments, children will have notes expressed in a manner that is most accessible to their own minds. They will find it much easier to review their notes later on for a test, because they will not have to relearn the material.

It is very important for children to review their notes *before* the next class, both to become familiar with the material and at the same time to begin to study for the next exam. By reviewing their notes soon after they have taken them, youngsters will be working with the material when it is still fresh in their minds and their grasp of it is strongest. If they wait a long time before reviewing the information, they will have considerable difficulty filling in the missing pieces of what the teacher said. As children review their notes, they will become more familiar with the material and begin to internalize it. Thoughts received in this manner have much greater residual power than those that emerge after a lengthy period of time. I can still remember much of the material I learned in school, even though I attended many years ago. As an astute person once said, "Education is what you have left after you have forgotten everything you ever learned."

It is very difficult to convince students of the importance of reviewing their class notes regularly. Although reviewing notes is an easy, straightforward task, many students turn it into a chore. Typically they find it laborious and unnecessary. This is particularly true of younger students because they usually have a substantial amount of homework to do, in the form of projects and reading and written assignments. These have to be handed in, whereas the teacher will not have any evidence that they are working hard to really learn the material by reviewing notes, until they take a test. This is where the big pay-off comes.

Parents should not be swayed when children say that they can review their lecture notes right before the next test and still master the material. In all likelihood, young-sters will have a hard time reading what they have writ-ten, and they may be surprised to find out that their notes do not make much sense. This is not the time to be figuring out what was supposed to have been learned some time ago. The result may be a devastating blow to self-confidence, which will be reflected in test results. Although it takes children a little more time in the short run to review their class notes, it will actually take less time in the long run to review them for a test. Their retention will be greater after they have already mastered the materials, so the review process will be quicker and easier.

The proper approach is to show children how to allot their time carefully so they are able to review class notes for all of their subjects before the next day in school, and still have time to complete all their reading and written assignments. Parents can be helpful in showing children how to develop a system that will enable them to get everything done on time and still have additional time left over for leisure activities. It all comes down to time management, and doing what one has to do, when one has to do it. I will give advice in the next section on time management techniques. The important point is that chil-dren cannot skimp on any of the steps in my system, because if they do they will not really be following it. Reviewing class notes is essential.

I rest my case with the following important statistics. Scientists have used experiments in information theory to show that the average person retains only about 20 percent of what he reads, 40 percent if he has heard it after reading it, and 60 percent if he also writes it down. Thus, even when children do all of the reading assignments, attend class regularly, listen carefully, and take good class notes, they will barely know enough to get a passing grade. By reviewing class notes regularly, children raise their retention level significantly above 60 percent.

The remaining steps in this section will show parents how to help children increase their mastery of the material to as close to the 100-percent mark as possible.

Principle 7
Parents should encourage children to review their notes before each class.

8

Preparing for Tests

Robert Louis Stevenson, the English author, once wrote, "Even if the doctor does not give you a year, even if he hesitates about a month, make one brave push and see what can be accomplished in a week." A lot can be accomplished in a week, particularly if one works continuously and diligently. One week is normally an adequate amount of time for children to prepare for most school examinations.

In reality, youngsters have been preparing for an exam much longer than a week if they have regularly reviewed their class notes and if they have kept up with their reading and written homework. If they have followed all of the steps I have suggested, they should have mastered material as it was presented to them. This does not mean, however, that they have sufficient command of the material to score high on a test. As time passes, the facts, concepts, and ideas that were very clear in our minds begin to fade. Even though there are remnants of this information in our memories, the longer the elapsed period of time since it was first presented, the hazier our understanding of it. Therefore, children need to conduct a thorough review of what they have learned immediately before a test.

Almost all teachers announce a schedule for examinations well in advance in order to give students ample opportunity to study. Some teachers, usually in the higher grades, provide their exam schedule at the beginning of the grading period. This gives students plenty of time to plan their schedules carefully. If teachers have not provided the exam schedule, then parents and their children need to seek it out—frequently if necessary.

There are some instructors who like to give unannounced quizzes to make sure that students are keeping up with their studies. Needless to say, this is not a popular practice, and it causes a lot of consternation for parents and students. Although I regard unannounced quizzes as a "dirty trick," children will be better prepared than their fellow students if they have been studying regularly.

To prepare adequately for an exam, elementary and junior-high-school students need to do three basic things: review their class notes, review (not reread) their reading assignments, and review their written assignments (particularly homework involving questions and problems). I will cover the review of class notes first, since teachers have an inclination to test students on material covered in class.

Reviewing class notes for a test should be a painless experience for children, if they have been reviewing and supplementing their notes continuously throughout the semester. At this point, the notes should be easy to read and all inconsistencies should have been resolved. The information is already ingrained in the children's minds, because they reviewed it earlier. All they need to do now is review the material sufficiently so they will have control over it for a test.

One week in advance of an announced test, I recommend that students start their review by reading their class notes at a leisurely pace. If they cannot cover all of their notes for this first review in one sitting, then they should pick up where they left off on the next day. They should not spend too much time and effort during this first review trying to master all of the concepts and inter-relationships in the material. In addition, they should not commit large blocks of information to memory at this point. The initial review is intended to be a refresher, and helps to build students' confidence that they have a basic understanding of the material that will be covered on the test. The next few phases of the review will help them gain complete mastery over the material.

The best way for students to master the material presented in class is to reread their class notes several times. After children have finished their first review of their notes, they still have five or six days left before an exam. After taking a short breather, they should start their second review, which youngsters should approach in a more active manner than the first. By this time they should be able to make clear distinctions between major and minor topics and understand important definitions. Parents can help children by having them recite the details noted under major points. If children are unable to retain details during this rehearsal, parents can help them tie this information in with other facts and relationships that they are already knowledgeable about. It is better if children can relate the information to their own personal experiences, because it will be easier to retain. Sometimes they can identify a few key words that will help trigger their memory about a whole body of knowledge.

Youngsters should find this second review to be considerably easier than the first. The second review is easier because the material is fresh in their minds from the first review, and they will now be able to anticipate the sequence of facts, ideas, and concepts. This review will help children internalize the material so they can reproduce or manipulate it at will. They should become more comfortable as they master the subjects, and their confidence will increase. A positive mental attitude is very important in helping to do well on examinations.

After children have finished the second review of their notes, they should then start their third review. By this time, they should almost be able to anticipate the content of the next page in their notes, not just the sequence of ideas. Most important, they should start to relate material in different sections of their notes, which often is what is required on examinations. From these reviews, children should become confident of their mastery of the material and may even begin to look forward to examinations so they can demonstrate their knowledge.

Youngsters can repeat this review process as many times as they want before a test. In general, the more reviews, the more complete their mastery of the material. A good general rule in preparing for any test is that children should review their class notes at least three times. On the other hand, parents and children should not become so obsessive that they feel the notes have to be reviewed ten times to master the material. Beyond some point, children will experience diminishing returns in their efforts because they have already gleaned most of the content from the material.

Here is one of my favorite poems about studying, taken from an old Elizabethan manuscript. I often quote it to college students:

> Multiplication is vexation,
> Division is as bad;
> The rule of three doth puzzle me,
> And practice drives me mad.

Whether the rule of three puzzles your children, or practice drives them mad, they are going to have to face up to the fact that they need to review their class notes several times. There is no other good way to learn the contents.

In addition to reading their class notes, students will also need to review reading and writing assignments in preparation for a test. In contrast to class notes, they should only need to review these assignments once, not three times. The review should serve as a refresher so they do not overlook any of this material. A student should not have to reread every single word of a reading assignment in preparation for a test. The idea is to read summary information, boldface type, major headings, key definitions, and so on, in the same manner as the techniques described earlier on how to preview a book before reading it. This exercise will help students remember the key information that they encountered when they first read the book.

It is also a good idea for students to review any written answers to homework problems relating to material that will be covered on the test. In particular, students should review the various math and science problems they did for homework or during class, because tests on these subjects often require similar approaches to solving problems. Students should make sure that they do not begin these reviews the night before the test, or they may not have time to complete everything at a leisurely pace. In general, the reviews should begin sometime during the week before a test.

Here are a few additional pointers that will help children prepare for tests:

Thinking about potential exam questions. It is impossible for children—or for that matter, parents—to guess all of the possible questions that will appear on an exam, since much of the obvious material is never tested. Nonetheless, it is still a good exercise for students to try to anticipate probable exam questions. This is not as difficult as it may seem, since many subjects group into certain major themes. It is easier for children to recognize these themes after reviewing their class notes, and reading and writing assignments.

Parents can also be of great assistance in helping children recognize likely exam questions. They can then ask their children hypothetical questions, and see how they would go about answering them. This helps children to organize the material in their minds and think about the sequence of points they might write on an exam.

It is also a good idea to have children recite answers out loud in their own words. Active rehearsal should help them to obtain a better grasp of the material and retain it longer. Rehearsing also gives children valuable experience in expressing themselves, which is what they will be required to do on an examination. This is a very good drill that will help them prepare for the real exam.

Rewriting graphs and equations. Certain subjects that elementary and junior-high-school students take, such as mathematics and science, rely heavily on symbols, equations, and graphs. Even if students review their notes several times and go over their homework problems, this may not be enough to give them total command over the subject. In such cases, they can supplement their review by rewriting the various symbols, equations, and graphs until they feel completely at ease with them. Students get good practice by writing mathematical expressions several times, and may find it easier to reproduce them on an exam. This exercise is particularly useful for graphing various curves and functions in mathematics, because it helps children remember the relationship of various lines and proper labels for the axes. They can practice writing these expressions on anything they choose, such as a blackboard, notebook paper, or even scrap paper.

Paying attention to materials the teacher distributes in class. Teachers will sometimes hand out additional reading materials to their students if the information is not covered in the textbook or they do not have time to go over it in class. It is important to impress upon children that the mere fact that the teacher gave out this information signifies its importance in the *teacher's* mind. Thus, they should treat this material as if it were actually presented by the teacher in class. This means that they should review it several times in preparation for a test, just as they will be doing with their class notes. Children should make sure that they can recognize the relationship between the material handed to them and the material the teacher has presented in class. Such information may figure prominently in examinations, so it is wise to be prepared. If the teacher has noted that certain parts of the readings will be intensively questioned on a test, then students may have to give this material more attention than the usual "once-over." In such cases, they may want to outline the relevant part of the readings and review this outline along with their class notes in preparation for a test.

Memorizing material for tests. Even though teachers are most interested in a student's abilities to understand material, they will still be required to memorize a number of things in some subjects. These things may include key principles, definitions, historical facts, and so on, depending upon the subject. In most cases, students should be able to commit material to memory by reviewing their notes and locking them into their memory while studying for an exam. If this does not suffice, then students may have to do some extra work.

The problem most students have is that they do not know how to go about memorizing information. Some just stare at the material for a lengthy period of time, hoping that they will somehow be able to absorb it. This is ineffective.

Here is a more effective approach that I often recommend to older students. Children can record information that they need to know on three-by-five index cards. They can write the word or principle to be memorized on one side of the card, and its meaning or other pertinent information on the other side. Then, during spare moments, they can glance at the front of the card and see if they can remember what is on the back of the card. Children can repeat this procedure as often as necessary until they retain the information.

Conducting an organized and continuous review. A one-week review before a test should be sufficient, but many students have a tendency to procrastinate. Parents should encourage children to conduct their review throughout the entire week rather than allow several days to elapse between reviews. This can prove difficult for children because they spend a good part of their day in school and may have extracurricular activities afterward. Youngsters need to understand that school is important, and that they must be diligent during such periods.

Continuous study is very important if children are to master a subject. They are able to learn subjects more quickly this way, because they do not have to go back and remember where they left off at their last reading.

It is best if children can study for at least a little while during each day of the week prior to an exam, not counting the day of the exam itself. In addition, they can usually accomplish much more by studying for a significant amount of time, rather than conducting their review in numerous small time intervals. The advantage of studying for lengthy periods of time is that they can begin to see the relationships between various ideas, theories, or principles. Younger children should not study for too long, however, or the effort will be counterproductive.

Knowing when to stop studying. The general rule: students should never study up to the last minute before an exam. If they have been studying hard during the week before an exam, it is best to exercise a little moderation and stop the day before—or at least a few hours before—they take the exam. Studying up to the last minute can be disconcerting. Children are much more likely to be self-confident if they do not have to cram everything into their heads in the final hours before taking a test. And they will need all of their energy and ingenuity to do well on the exam. The importance of rest for growing children cannot be overemphasized. They need to be relaxed and mentally sharp in order to perform up to their full potential.

Here is some advice for parents whose children are concerned that they will forget a lot of information by the time of the test if they started studying a week in advance. Tell your youngsters that if they really understand ideas and their interrelationships rather than isolated bits of information, then their retention of the material should be very good. They should be able to retain the information even more effectively if they were able to relate it to some particular aspect of their own lives.

I have one final bit of advice on studying. Some study guides recommend that students prepare for exams by working in study groups, if they can find some knowledgeable people who are willing to do their share of the work. I feel that this approach is a disadvantage to students who are well-prepared, because they end up spending their time trying to educate others who are not prepared. Students who use the study methods I have described will definitely be in the well-prepared group. Therefore, I discourage participation in study groups unless specifically requested by the teacher. Studying is basically a solitary endeavor, not a social affair. Taking exams is certainly a solitary task, because the other people in the study group will not be there to help your child; if they are, it is called cheating.

Parents, if you want your children to do well on exams, you must encourage them to study. Don't let them think for a minute that they might get lucky and do well on an exam without studying. Remember what Louis Pasteur said: "In the fields of observation, chance favors only the mind that is prepared."

Principle 8
Parents should encourage their children to start studying for exams a full week in advance.

9

Taking Tests and Scoring High

Charles Colton, a nineteenth-century author, said, "Examinations are formidable even to the best prepared, for the greatest fool may ask more than the wisest man can answer." Although this is a true statement, we should also recognize that there are certain skills in taking tests that anyone can learn. In this chapter I will show parents how to help their children become test-wise, so they can score high on different types of exams.

The first thing to teach children is that testing is one of the "facts of life" and that they will have to contend with it for the rest of their lives. In the broadest sense, we are all tested continuously on practically everything we do. When children are infants, parents test them to see when they can walk and talk. As they get older, they are tested not only in school by their teachers but also at home by their parents. We test them on how well they can play sports on the athletic field. When they become adults, they will be examined by their supervisor on how well they can complete an assigned project. Even parents who stay at home are tested on how well they can carry out their family responsibilities. In the broadest sense, testing is one of those facts of life that begins in the cradle and follows us to the grave. The sooner children recognize this fact, the better they will be able to cope with taking tests.

Even more important, testing determines how well your children do in school, whether they will get into college, and what kind of opportunities will be available to them later on. They will be required to take several exams in every course they study. These tests are like a turnstile that they must pass through to get to the next grade, to graduate from high school, to enter and finish college, and possibly to get a good job. Despite the prevalence of tests in our society, most people do not know how to take them. This should not come as a surprise, because schools are much better at giving exams than teaching students the proper way to take them. The ability to take a variety of tests and score high on them is an acquired skill, not an innate ability.

In this chapter, I will discuss the approaches that children should use for taking different types of tests. My review will cover the tests typically given in elementary and junior high school. These tests include essay exams (written responses), objective exams (such as multiple choice, true-false), and problem exams (in mathematics and science). I will not cover other types of tests that students usually encounter later on, such as open-book, take-home, comprehensive, and oral exams. I discuss the techniques for taking these types of tests in my other study guide, *Getting Straight A's*. Finally, I will not cover the methods used to take more general exams, such as I.Q. and aptitude tests, and various standardized exams. Before turning to the methods children should use to take each type of exam, I present a few basic principles they should follow before taking any test.

Basic Principles Before Taking a Test

Always arrive on time. Advise children to arrive well ahead of time before taking a test. It is always disconcerting if they have to hurry or arrive late. This may cause them to lose their composure, or even to lose valuable time needed to complete the test.

Bring plenty of supplies. Parents should make sure that their children are well-stocked with the supplies they will need to take a test. This includes (sharpened) pencils, erasers, enough paper, exam booklets, and any special equipment, such as rulers, calculators, or compasses. Children may well find it unsettling to borrow supplies from their classmates—particularly if they do not have them.

Do not listen to other students before a test. When children arrive early to take an exam, they may hear their classmates talk about probable exam questions and their answers. They should not listen to this discussion. It is too late for them to add anything to their knowledge, and such conversation will only confuse or disarm them. It is better if they put some distance between themselves and the other students.

Read and listen to the instructions. The most common mistake made by students of all ages is to lunge right into an exam without reading and listening to the instructions. Children need to listen carefully to the teacher's verbal instructions and pay particular attention to any general written instructions on the exam paper. The instructions will tell them a number of important things, such as which questions to answer, the order in which the questions should be answered, what the teacher expects in the way of an answer, and the number of points assigned to each question. Students who are too anxious to get into an exam may end up answering the wrong questions, making it very difficult for them to get a good grade.

Be sure to write your name on the exam paper. If children do not do this, then the teacher may end up giving their good grade to someone else.

These are all very basic principles, and I am sure that parents and students have heard them a thousand times. Nonetheless, some of these principles have probably been violated on every test ever taken. Make sure that children have them engraved in their minds.

Essay Exams

While essay exams have always been given by teachers at the higher grade levels, they are now increasingly employed by teachers at the lower grade levels. This kind of exam tests a student's real mastery of a subject. An essay exam not only measures the ability to recall information, but also demonstrates the student's skill in analyzing, interpreting, and applying this information in an organized and logical manner. By revealing a student's reasoning behind an answer, the degree of his or her real understanding is displayed. At the same time, an essay exam encourages creativity and the organization of ideas, and it measures the student's ability to express these ideas in a thoughtful and well-written answer.

You are probably wondering how children should go about writing a good answer to an essay question. If you think that they should just come up with an answer and write it down then you are wrong. Much more is involved if they hope to do it right. In order to illustrate the mechanics of writing a good answer to an essay question, we will go through each of the steps from beginning to end for a hypothetical test.

Let's say that students have just been given an essay exam in one of their classes. The way they spend the first five minutes or so on the test will determine which questions they will answer, how well they will answer them, and how well they will do on the test. Students should spend those minutes looking over the exam very carefully. They should notice how many questions and pages are in the exam, and they should read each question carefully before answering any one of them. As they read each question, they should ask themselves what is being requested. Is the teacher looking for a recitation of facts, an understanding of ideas and their interrelationships, an application of basic principles, or what? Children should underline the key words in the question that tell them specifically what they are supposed to do. Are they supposed to discuss or describe, to compare or contrast, to develop or demonstrate? While these instructions may sound very similar, they are really quite different. Included in my appendix is a list of key words that are often used in essay exams, and what they mean. Make sure your child reads them at some point.

It is important for youngsters to have a complete understanding of the test questions if they have any hope of answering them properly. If students do not comprehend every aspect of a test question, they should ask the teacher for a clarification. Most teachers are receptive to such inquiries.

As children read each question, they should jot down words or thoughts that come to mind as part of the answer. They should make these notes in the margin of the test paper next to each question. It is not necessary to write complete thoughts, only a few words that will serve as a reminder. They should read every essay question on the test in this manner before attempting to answer any one of them. There are three good reasons for doing this. First, they will know what will be required of them on the test. Second, sometimes the essay questions are related to each other. Third, by knowing the questions up front, their minds can work on an answer subconsciously throughout the entire exam. This will increase the likelihood that they will come up with a good response when they answer the question.

After youngsters have read each question and jotted down their thoughts, they need to decide which queries to answer and how much time to allot to each one. By putting down their thoughts, they should now know which questions they are most knowledgeable about. If they have a choice, they should naturally select the questions that will be the easiest for them, not the most challenging. They should also plan to devote an amount of time to each question that is proportional to its total point score. For example, if they are taking a one-hour test with one 50-point question and two 25-point questions, then they should devote a half hour to the first question and fifteen minutes to each of the other two. If they have a choice of order, children should always answer the easiest questions first and return to the more difficult questions later on. This will give them confidence because they have already completed the easy questions, and will allow more time for their minds to work on a subconscious level to come up with a good answer.

Students are now ready to start writing an answer to the question they have decided to answer first. At this point, they have a few thoughts written in the margin of the test paper that they will include in the answer. They should now supplement these thoughts with any other information that they have been able to come up with. The next step is to write a number beside each thought in the margin in the order that it will appear in the answer. This is similar to constructing an outline, in an informal way. In writing the answer to the essay question, a good general rule is that it should have a beginning, middle, and end. The beginning should clearly state the thesis or theme of the essay. The middle should contain a development of this thesis. Each paragraph should include evidence, arguments, or reasons to support the thesis. Major facts and ideas should be supported by specific examples and details. It helps if the student demonstrates the proper use of technical terms and repeats some of the wisdom imparted by the teacher in the classroom. And finally, the end should summarize the thesis and conclude that it has been demonstrated. All of the other essay questions should be answered in the same manner.

Here are some additional pointers that will help students to write good answers to essay questions. The first and most basic principle is that they should answer *only* the question asked and not the question they would *like* to answer. It doesn't do any good to write a long answer if it is the wrong answer. Second, if students encounter a difficult question that they do not immediately know how to answer, they should not give up. One possible alternative is to break up complex questions into manageable parts and approach them from a different direction. Third, even if students are having a lot of difficulty, they should at least write something. This may help them to connect with a memory chain, in which one thought reminds them of another thought, and so on. Fourth, if students have an absolute block in answering a question, they should leave adequate space and come back to it later on. This will give their minds additional time to work on the answer on a subconscious level. And finally, if students run out of time in answering an essay question, they should provide a brief outline for the part they were unable to complete. An outline demonstrates to the teacher that they know the answer, and should earn some points.

Objective Exams

Objective exams are very popular at the elementary and junior-high-school levels. These types of exams include true-false, fill in the blanks, multiple choice, matching questions, or some combination. Generally speaking, an exam is objective if the same standards and conditions apply to everyone taking the test, and there is only one "right" answer to the question. Objective tests primarily measure a student's ability to recall information but, if properly designed, they can also test the ability to understand, analyze, interpret, and apply knowledge. These tests are popular with teachers because they are straightforward, often standardized, easy to grade, and require less work on their part.

The basic principles for taking objective tests are a little different from the points I covered on essay exams. At the start, students should take a few minutes to look over the exam to see the number of questions and pages, but they should not try to read all of the questions before marking their answers. The best approach is to answer the questions in the order they appear on the exam. When students encounter a difficult question, they should leave it blank, mark it with a question mark, and move on to the next query. They can always return to these questions at a later point, after they have finished the easier ones. The difficult questions may even be more manageable at this point, since children have had additional time to think about them on a subconscious level. Moreover, there is always the possibility that they may find information in other questions that will help them answer the more difficult queries. Parents should caution children not to be superstitious about the pattern of responses in objective exams. For example, they should not be influenced by a pattern like T, F, T, F, T, F, . . . on a true-false test, or a, b, c, a, b, c, . . . on a multiple choice exam.

Here are some basic principles students should observe when taking objective exams. These exams often present a challenge because there are several possible answers to choose from, and more than one of them seems plausible.

The best approach is for students to try to determine the correct answer before looking at the options in the question. Even if they see the answer they guessed, they should still examine the other options to make sure that none of these seem closer to the truth than the one they initially decided on. If students do not know the answer beforehand, they should read each of the options very carefully and eliminate the responses they know to be incorrect. Thus, even if they do not know the answer, they may arrive at it by a process of elimination.

Many students have difficulty with objective exams because they have certain preconceptions about them. These feelings often come from a false belief in the naïveté of the teacher, which may not be accurate. For example, some people would advise students to avoid options that use words like *always*, *never*, *all*, *none*, *must*, *only*, and so forth, because nothing in the world is so exclusive. On the other hand, they advise students to select options that allow for some exception, such as *usually*, *seldom*, *sometimes*, *frequently*, *rarely*, *often*, and so on. Some people think you should avoid the first or last option, because teachers feel more comfortable about putting the correct answer in the middle. Some others even tell students to select the option that is shorter or longer than the rest, because it is more likely to be true. Still another popular belief is that students should never change their answer, because their first intuition is likely to be correct. While there may be a grain of truth in some of this folk wisdom, it is basically superstition and students should put no faith in it.

Here is some additional advice that students *should* follow on objective exams. If they have gone all of the way through a test and still do not know the answers to some of the questions, then they should guess. If they skip over the question, they will surely miss it. If they guess, there is at least a chance of being correct. The odds are very good on a true-false test (50–50), and a little less on a multiple choice exam (depending upon the number of options). Even if the teacher has assigned a penalty for being wrong—by subtracting points—it still pays for the student to guess if the penalty is small enough.

Problem Exams

Elementary and junior-high-school students will encounter plenty of problem tests in school, especially in quantitative disciplines such as mathematics and science. Teachers start using problem tests at a very early age because they develop a student's ability to use logical reasoning to find solutions. Many students have a mental block, commonly known as "math anxiety," about mathematics in any form. These students "freeze-up" at the thought of having to solve a math problem or take a math test. Students' ability in mathematics is tied to their ability to reason abstractly, which, to some degree, is innate. On the other hand, just about all students are capable of doing mathematics satisfactorily if they know how to approach the subject. Success will depend partly on learning mathematics in a very progressive and orderly fashion, as I described earlier in the chapter on arithmetic. But success also depends on developing an aptitude for taking problem tests, and that is the subject here.

Several basic principles will help children score higher on problem tests. As with essay exams, students should read through all of the questions on problem tests before attempting to answer any one of them. As students read each question, they should underline key words that tell them what to do—they need to know what is requested of them before they can solve the problem. They should also underline important data, such as given information, units of amount, and so on.

In the margin of the test paper, students should also jot down any thoughts that will help them solve the problem later on, such as specific formulae, simplifying substitutions, or other approaches. They should then move to the next problem and continue with the same procedure. After they have previewed all of the problems on the test in the same manner, they will then have an idea of the problems that will be relatively easy and those that could cause some difficulty. If students have a choice, they should select the problems that will be the easiest and figure out how much time they have to work on each one. As with the advice on essay exams, they should solve the easiest problems first and save the more difficult ones until later, to give themselves more time to work on an answer subconsciously.

As children go back to solve each problem, they should make sure that they have an exact understanding of what is being requested. Here are some tips on how to do this. They should first list all of the unknowns that they are supposed to solve in the problem. Sometimes it is helpful to organize all of the given information in a table, or draw a diagram that maps out what they need to do to solve the problem. A good strategy is to try to predict a reasonable answer to the problem before working on it, to provide a basis for comparison later on. Children should always show all of their work on problem exams, rather than trying to make complex computations in their heads. This way, if they make a silly mistake and get the wrong answer, the teacher can at least see where they went wrong and give them partial credit. Instruct children to be very careful and deliberate in their calculations, to reduce the number of computational errors. When they derive an answer, they should check to make sure that it meets all of the requirements of the problem. Finally, when they have finished their work, they should draw a box around the answer to make it easier for the teacher to locate.

I will now provide an example of this approach to solve a simple problem. If I know that a rectangle has a perimeter of 30 feet and a width of 5 feet; what is its length? The first thing that should register in my mind is that the unknown value I want to find is the length (l). I then note that I am given two pieces of information: the perimeter (p = 30 feet) and the width (w = 5 feet). At this point, I will draw a picture of the rectangle to get a visual representation of it, and fill in the given information and unknown value:

Length (l)

Width (w) = 5 feet   Perimeter (P) = 30 feet

Now it is clear that to solve this problem, all I need to do is write down the formula for finding the perimeter of a rectangle, substitute in all of the given information, and solve for its length (l). I also mentally note that since the perimeter of a rectangle is two times the length plus two times the width, the length should be more than 5 feet but less than 15 feet. I now carry out the calculations very carefully:

Write the formula and insert the given information	Rearrange the equation to solve for 1.
$P = 2l + 2w$	$30 = 2l + 10$
$30 = 2(l) + 2(5)$	$30 - 10 = 2l$
	$20 = 2l$ or $\boxed{l = 10 \text{ feet}}$

This tells me that the length of the rectangle is 10 feet. I note that my answer falls in the range I predicted, and meets all of the requirements of the problem. (For example, if I plug the value of l = 10 feet back into the formula, I can see that my answer checks out.) I have shown all of my work so the instructor can see exactly what I have done, in case I have made a careless error. Finally, I draw a box around my answer so it will be easy for the teacher to locate. At this point I am ready to move on to the next problem.

Even if children do all of these things, they will sometimes encounter problems that are difficult to solve. In such cases, they may need to approach the problem in a different way. Since many teachers include problems similar to homework on a test, students should think about the approaches they used to solve these problems. Sometimes there is a clever substitution or particular approach that makes math problems easier to solve. Just as "there is more than one way to skin a cat," there is often more than one way to solve a problem—and usually several wrong ways, as well. Students may approach a problem from a different angle to get a solution. The main thing is that they need to keep working at the problem, because a correct answer exists. Even if a student only knows how to solve part of a problem she should write it down; at least she will get partial credit.

As students progress to higher grades they will encounter other types of tests, such as open book, take-home, oral, and comprehensive written exams. Since these tests are rarely given in elementary and junior high school, I do not plan to cover them here. Parents interested in learning about the techniques for taking these other types of tests should consult my study guide designed for older students, *Getting Straight A's*.

Next I will discuss the basic principles to follow while taking a test. Even though you have been told about them many times before, they are often violated. Read them very carefully and make sure that your child understands these fundamental rules.

Basic Principles While Taking a Test

Write answers clearly. Many young children have difficulty with their handwriting, but they can increase the odds of doing well on exams by writing their answers very clearly. They should go out of their way to write neatly and organize their responses very carefully. The teacher is more likely to understand what children write if they use good penmanship, and practice the rules of good grammar, accurate spelling, logical paragraph construction, and sound theme development. The result is often a higher grade from the teacher. One teacher told me that he added five extra points to my exam score because I had written my answers so neatly. Parents may also want to encourage their children to use a pencil rather than a pen on exams, so they can erase parts of their answer if they change their minds. This makes for a neater paper.

Some students think the teacher may give them the benefit of the doubt if their paper is hard to read. Contrary to what they think, bad or sloppy handwriting only gives the impression that they do not know the complete answer to the problem. Moreover, the teacher is more likely to miss the part of an answer that the student does know if the writing is illegible. Teachers have a hard enough time grading all of the papers for students in the class. Your child can ease the burden somewhat by writing clearly and neatly. Although this requires more work and care, it is well worth the extra effort.

Review answers very carefully. When children finish answering the questions on an exam ahead of time, they should go back and review their answers very carefully. It is very easy to make careless mistakes when writing rapidly, and children often make more mistakes than adults because they have had less experience writing.

Even when children try to be careful, their essays may contain faulty spelling, poor grammar, incomplete paragraph construction, illegible writing, and so forth. They may have made silly clerical errors on an objective test. Or they may have been guilty of a logical error or computational mistake on a problem exam. It is possible to catch many of these careless errors by carefully reviewing answers a second time.

In just about every examination I have ever taken, there have been some students who finish ahead of the others and turn in their papers before the time is up. Sometimes they do not know all of the answers, and other times they seem to be announcing to the teacher and the rest of the class that the test was a snap. On occasion you can even hear them out in the hallway complaining that they forgot to write certain parts of an answer that they knew well. That mistake could have been avoided if only they had remained in class and reviewed their exam papers another time. It is silly for students not to use all of the time a teacher allows to take a test. Any product made by man can be improved with additional effort, and an exam is no exception. Parents should encourage their children to continue working on a test until *all* of the time is used up.

Never cheat on an exam. I'm sure that all parents have told their children about the pitfalls of cheating. Unfortunately, some children cheat on tests by using "crib sheets"—some even write the answers on their hands and arms—or looking for answers on their classmates' papers. For one thing, parents should teach their children that it is unwise to cheat because they may get caught and either flunk the course or even be expelled from school. Moreover, when children cheat, they implicitly assume that someone else knows a better answer than they do. If children have been following the system I have laid out in this book, they should know as much as anyone in the classroom. A final reason for not cheating is that students will not truly accomplish anything if they do not earn their grades fairly. There is a far more practical and productive approach than cheating:

Principle 9
Parents should teach their children the methods for taking various types of exams so they will be test-wise.

10

Showing The Teacher
What You Have Learned

John Lyly, an English author, once said, "Let me stand to the main chance." An examination is the main chance for students to show the teacher what they have learned from their studies. If they have followed the advice in earlier chapters, they should have mastered the material and also know the best strategies for taking different types of tests. This chapter provides additional pointers on taking tests, so students can "stand to the main chance."

Most teachers use tests to make sure that children have *really* mastered the material. Sometimes in the lower grades children are asked to supply a straightforward recitation of the material they have learned. But the better teachers usually ask their students to do more than regurgitate the material verbatim on the exam. The most effective tests ask students to apply the information they have learned to solve a new problem. This may require them to combine the information in ways that were not specifically discussed by the teacher in class. After all, this is similar to what they will have to do when they get into the real world, because most problems are not neat textbook cases. Tests that require children to combine and apply information teach them how to think, and this will help them not only in the classroom but also later in life.

Just as skilled craftsmen must know how to use the tools of their trade, students must understand and know how to use tools needed to solve particular problems. "Tools" are especially important in certain courses, such as mathematics and the physical sciences. Obtaining the right answer in these subjects usually requires selection of the right formulas and proper application of them.

Parents should advise their children to go into an exam with a completely open mind. When taking a test, they should not try to force their responses into a mold that fits their readings or their notes. The teacher may be testing whether they can apply their knowledge in a different way. Students need to realize that sometimes they have to move out of their ordinary way of thinking and be creative to come up with good answers to questions. If they have studied their notes and readings very diligently during the week prior to a test, they have loaded a wide assortment of information into their minds. They will be working with this information subconsciously during the period before a test, exploring the interrelationships between various facts, principles, and ideas. All of this preparation should put them in a creative mood for the test.

Students tend to do better on exams when they have the proper mental attitude and a high degree of self-confidence. I have heard many coaches talk about the importance of confidence when competing in an athletic event. Athletes who are confident are able to perform at their highest level, which gives them an advantage over their competitors. Taking an exam is not too different from an athletic event, because your child will be competing against the other students in the class. In a sense, students are even competing against themselves, because they are trying to get as close to perfection as possible in filling out their answers. As in an athletic event, they should set their sights high and work as hard as possible to reach the pinnacle. If we can generate the same degree of intensity in the classroom that we often see on the playing field, our children will find education to be a much more rewarding experience.

In contrast to self-confidence, fear has a detrimental effect on a student's ability to perform on an exam. Some people experience fear and anxiety even at the thought of having to take an exam. They become very nervous, worried, and even ill because they are afraid that they might fail. Many youngsters worry about the catastrophic repercussions that will befall them if they do poorly on a test. They worry most about the criticism and ridicule that will come from their parents, but they also worry about what their teachers or classmates will think of them. Some people become anxious about taking a test merely because they have invested a lot in preparing for it, and feel that they have to do well to justify their efforts. People who worry about how they are going to do—for whatever reason—often become nervous. In fact they are so worried about doing poorly that their ability becomes impaired and they unwittingly bring about the very thing that they were anxious about.

Most of the fears and anxieties I have described plague children because they lack self-confidence. The youngsters who tend to fall into this syndrome have done poorly in the past and, thus, do not have much confidence in their ability to prepare for a test. One of the advantages of the system I have presented is that it will enable children to study more effectively and make higher grades, thus increasing their self-confidence that they can do even better in the future. As they experience more and more success over time in taking exams, their fears should start to dissipate because they will know that they have done everything possible to reach their potential.

Parents can also provide assistance in helping their children to overcome the fear of taking exams. The assistance comes in the form of explaining to children what tests are really all about. Examinations give parents and teachers a quantitative assessment of children's knowledge about a particular subject, and indicate where improvement is needed. It is important for children to understand that tests are basically a learning device for them. They are not an assessment of the intrinsic worth of individuals, but merely an assessment of how much they know about a particular subject at a given time. Examinations are less threatening to children when viewed in this manner. Children should never have low self-esteem because they have performed poorly on a test. They must understand that sooner or later, everyone makes mistakes. Their goal should be to make the mistakes before the exam, learn from them, and avoid repeating them on the exam.

Another way for children to become more comfortable with exams is learning where they went wrong on a test. When most teachers return an exam to their students, they review the questions and explain what was required for a good answer. Children should listen carefully to these explanations so they can avoid repeating their mistakes on the next test, the final, or in the next course. This should help them appreciate that when we learn from our mistakes, we are setting the stage for further growth.

Children will do better on exams if they know some things about their teachers. Although most teachers ask different questions from class to class and year to year, they exhibit a certain style in the type and scope of questions they ask on a test. I encourage older students to figure out a teacher's M.O. (modus operandi), or behavior patterns, to anticipate how they deal with subjects. Although this may prove too much of a challenge for younger students, there are certain things they can do. After your child takes a first test from a teacher, you should help him or her to analyze the situation. For example, did the teacher use an essay, objective, or problem exam? What kinds of questions did the teacher ask, and was the emphasis on memorizing facts, understanding ideas, or applying principles? Did the teacher seek an understanding of major themes or a mastery of minutiae? Helping children understand the types of questions teachers ask will help them to prepare for the next test or the final.

Children will also have a better perspective about exams if parents explain how they are graded. In some classes there are set cutoffs for different grades, such as 90–100 for an A, 80–89 for a B, 70–79 for a C, and so forth. In other classes, however, teachers award grades in a manner that approximates the normal distribution in statistics. In other words, a certain proportion of students will get the highest grades, most will be in the broad middle-range, and only a few will get the lowest grades. Thus, the grade a student gets depends mostly on how the other students did, and not the absolute point score they received. The competition will be much tougher when the other students in the class are very sharp. On the other hand, if the other students are not very sharp, they will fill out the lower end of the grading curve.

Even though it helps children to know how they will be graded, it is still important for them to understand that grading exams is a subjective and fickle affair. The grade children receive may depend in part on how well other students performed whose papers have already been graded, since this helps create a certain standard in some teachers' minds. Moreover, some teachers place greater emphasis on certain parts of an answer than others, such as grammar, spelling, handwriting, an understanding of the ideas, how the argument is organized and presented, how much the teacher thinks the student really knows based on classroom participation, and probably a number of other factors as well. The key consideration is what the teacher *thinks* is important, and this is also something that can be learned through experience.

Taking Final Exams

The advice I have offered applies to any exam, but there are some special things students can do to prepare for final exams. The first task is to find out exactly which subjects will be covered on the finals. Most teachers are candid about describing the material for which they will hold students responsible on the final. A specific question to ask is whether the final will cover only material since the last exam or for the entire term or year. This is an important question because the answer will determine how they should prepare for the final. If the final covers only material since the last exam, then students should study for it in the same manner as for any other exam. On the other hand, if the final covers the entire course, then students should review materials beginning with the first class. This is not as difficult as it may sound, because students should already be familiar with the earlier material if they have been following my study methods.

One of the toughest things students have to deal with is facing the heavy workload around the time finals are given. A student taking five or six subjects may have to take a final exam in each of them. To prepare adequately, students should take a close look at their schedule about one month before the school term is over to determine exactly when finals will occur. They can then work backward from each exam to determine when they should start studying. A student facing several finals may need to start studying a few weeks before each exam is given, rather than the customary one-week period recommended earlier.

Students should use a slightly different approach to prepare for finals than they used in studying for regular exams. While regular exams typically test specialized knowledge about a subject, final exams often cover generalized knowledge or major themes that run through various topics studied during the year. When students prepare for final exams, they need to look for these major themes. This should not be too difficult if they have been following my study methods, because they will already have mastered and retained the material presented earlier in the year. All they need to do after identifying the major themes is to have some knowledge about the specific details associated with them.

As children start studying for their final exams, parents should encourage them to review regular exams that the teacher gave earlier in the year. Although it is unlikely that the teacher will ask the same questions on the final, your child may see a pattern in the type of questions asked by the teacher. Make sure that your youngster understands the answers to all questions on previous exams, because final exams often review similar material again. Children can prepare ahead of time by taking good notes when the teacher reviews earlier exams and describes what constitutes a good answer. The objective is for children to go into a final exam with complete mastery of everything presented during the year, and avoid repeating previous mistakes.

Children's frame of mind during finals will be an important determinant of their performance. They need to prepare adequately so they will be able to take their exams in a confident and relaxed manner. It is very important that they use their time wisely to study, because it will slip away very quickly if they are not vigilant. It is certainly true that finals are very important because they are the last signal to the teacher about how much the student has learned. Nonetheless, students should not worry about the fact that the final is the most significant exam of the year. If they have been following the study methods I have described here, they will be well-prepared and the final will be no more difficult than any other test.

Principle 10
Parents should explain the nature of exams to their children so they will be confident and self-assured when they take them.

SUMMARY

Part 3
A System for Getting Good Grades

PRINCIPLE 1
Plan a course of study for children, and work hard to keep them on the right track.

PRINCIPLE 2
You must work effectively with teachers for your child to succeed in school.

PRINCIPLE 3
Don't allow children to miss class unless they are genuinely too ill to attend.

PRINCIPLE 4
Make sure that children sit in the front row of the class.

PRINCIPLE 5
Make sure that children complete all homework assignments before attending class.

PRINCIPLE 6
Encourage your child to take extensive notes during class.

PRINCIPLE 7
Parents should encourage children to review their notes before each class.

PRINCIPLE 8
Parents should encourage their children to start studying for exams a full week in advance.

PRINCIPLE 9
Parents should teach their children the methods for taking various types of exams so they will be test-wise.

PRINCIPLE 10
Parents should explain the nature of exams to their children so they will be confident and self-assured when they take them.

MAKING THE SYSTEM WORK FOR YOUR CHILD

1

Study Tips

Students will have a much easier time following all of the steps I have provided in the previous section if they have developed good study habits. I have a favorite poem that I advise older students to learn as an aid to acquiring good study habits. The poem is also appropriate for younger students. The poet is Rudyard Kipling, and the poem is called *The Elephant's Child*:

> I keep six honest serving men
> (They taught me all I knew);
> Their names are What and Why and When
> And How and Where and Who.

You will not need to ask two of the serving men "Who" will be studying (your child) and "Why" it is important to study (otherwise, you would not be reading this book). We will see what the other four serving men have to say about practicing good study habits.

When to Study

It is a good idea for parents to encourage their children to do at least some studying every day. This does not mean that they need to study the same amount each day, but they should do at least some work so that they can continue to make progress. When children do nothing for several days, the amount of work starts piling up, they fall further behind, and the task becomes unpleasant. That is why studying is so distasteful to some children.

Parents need to help children schedule their time, but they should guard against going too far with this approach. Some parents develop elaborate calendars that tell their youngsters what they are supposed to be doing during every minute, hour, and day of the year. These calendars allocate time periods for studying each subject, playing with friends, participating in athletic events, eating meals, and so forth. Personally, I feel that this approach goes too far, because it does not allow for any freedom or the development of self-reliance. Children will not accept such regimentation for very long, and are likely to become bored with their studies and rebel. Parents should use calendars for their intended purpose, which is to record *significant* dates. Write down the dates when children have to take exams, complete projects, and turn in papers, but do not use calendars to regulate their lives!

When planning a schedule for children to complete their work, parents need to look ahead for only a few days at a time. The tasks youngsters must complete during that time are obvious. They will need to review and supplement their notes from class, complete reading and writing assignments before the next class, prepare for an exam if one is coming up, and work on term papers or other projects if they have been assigned. Parents should help their children to allocate their time in a manner to get all of these tasks done, and still have time left over for other activities. By planning for only a couple of days at one stretch, it is possible to make changes in the schedule for the most efficient use of time.

Children face many competing demands, so the challenge for parents is to show them how to complete everything in an orderly manner. For example, if children have extracurricular activities at certain times, they may need to do schoolwork during other hours. But parents should make sure that their youngsters are not involved in too many extracurricular activities—or too tired after these activities—because their studies may suffer. The key to completing everything on time is for children to make the best use of available time, and to do schoolwork during periods when they might be watching television or playing video games. If children use small time periods wisely, they can accomplish a lot. Another good strategy is for children to use portions of weekends or holidays to catch up on their studies. But they should never study for so long that there is no time for leisure, or this will turn studying into drudgery.

Where to Study

Many parents insist that their children study in certain locations. This is often a mistake. Children should be able to study anywhere they choose, as long as they are comfortable there and can accomplish a significant amount of work. Some children prefer to study in the library, others in a particular chair or room, and some may even like to study in bed. Among my three children, each has a favorite spot to study—and fortunately, they are not all in the same place. The important point is that children prefer a particular spot because they can work diligently and block out distractions when they are there. No single best study place exists for all individuals, so parents need to give their children some leeway.

In selecting a place to study, children must be able to concentrate for an extended period of time. Students who have problems with concentration often become fatigued after even a half hour of studying. Some people seem to be able to concentrate in the noisiest of surroundings, while others are distracted by even the slightest sound. Even though many people can adjust to the noise level in a room, it is often more disturbing if the room changes alternately between quiet and noisy. Many people are distracted more by their own frame of mind than by what is going on in the room. For example, if people are in a room that is supposed to be quiet, like a library, they often become distracted if other people are talking. With some extra effort and concentration, it is often possible to screen out noises that would otherwise be distracting. Parents can be very helpful by showing children how to focus their powers of concentration.

Youngsters also need to realize that there are places to study other than their favorite study spot. They can mentally review the new concepts they have learned while performing everyday activities such as getting dressed, eating meals, riding the school bus, and so forth. Parents can assist in this effort, by helping their children to review what they have learned at the dinner table or while traveling. The main idea is to make a game out of these sessions, in the same manner as quiz shows that test the contestants' knowledge.

What to Study

Even though children will know what subjects they must study if they have planned their schedule appropriately, they will also need to be specific in their efforts. For example, your child will have to select which subjects he will study, and in what order. He will also need to decide such things as the number of pages he will read in his social studies book, how much of his English paper he will attempt to write, how many mathematics problems he will attempt to solve, and so on. Children need to challenge themselves to complete not only the amount of work they are required to do, but to exceed these limits if possible. By working hard each day, they should see some real progress and experience a sense of accomplishment as well.

I think it is easier for students to decide on how much they want to achieve rather than how much time they will spend on each subject or activity. When children think about how much time they will spend on each subject, they are more likely to end up watching the clock instead of concentrating on their studies. The only caution here is that they should not try to accomplish so much in one subject—perhaps a favorite subject—that there is little time left to complete their other work.

Students should also alternate the order of subjects they are studying, to add some variety to their work. One approach is to alternate between subjects that are quantitative and nonquantitative. For example, after studying a subject that requires problem solving, like science or math, they may want to read a chapter from their English or history book. Children can also alternate studying between subjects they find interesting and tedious. For example, if a child likes English but dislikes mathematics, she might read part of a novel after solving mathematics problems. Making these substitutions helps children study for a longer period of time without getting bored or taking overly long rest periods.

It is important to teach children that they should never neglect a subject because they find it boring and tedious. All of the subjects children study in school are needed to produce well-rounded individuals. If children neglect key courses, such as English or mathematics, they may eventually do poorly in other subjects that require these skills. Moreover, they may fall so far behind in courses they neglect that it becomes practically impossible to salvage the course with a good grade. And it only becomes more difficult when they take more advanced courses in a subject if they never learned the basic material.

How to Study

Children should always approach studying with the right frame of mind. Before sitting down to study, they should decide whether they really want to study at this time or do something else. If they have something else to do—such as participating in a worthwhile extracurricular activity—then it may be wise to postpone studying until a later time. But parents should never allow their children to procrastinate merely because they dislike studying or want to participate in an activity that is not worthwhile. They will have to study anyway at a later time and, at this point, the work may get in the way of something else that is worthwhile. Part of growing up is developing the self-discipline to do what one has to do, when one has to do it, and the sooner children learn this basic lesson the more manageable their lives will be.

Studying will prove easier for children if parents can get them to "throw themselves" into their work, and not let anything interfere with their thought processes. Youngsters will do their best when they approach their studies with enthusiasm, determination, and sincerity. When children find it difficult to sit down and study, start them on some relatively easy aspect that will enable them to ease gradually into their work. Students often become more enthusiastic about their studies when they find out that the task is easier than they first thought.

When doing their studies, children should only attempt to concentrate on one thing at a time. They should not try to work on two subjects simultaneously. And, in particular, they should not watch television, play video games, or converse with their friends while attempting to study. It is not possible to accomplish two separate activities efficiently at the same time.

Although children often become distracted, they will accomplish much more if they work continuously over an extended period of time. When youngsters do so, they do not have to keep going back to find out where they left off from their last sitting. Moreover, they will be able to see the relationships between various ideas and concepts more clearly if they stick with their studies for a period of time. This does not mean that they have to spend all day studying, but they can accomplish a lot if they study for a few hours at a time. The general rule is that children should always spend enough time with their studies, but never so much that the whole experience becomes grueling and boring.

When children study for an extended period of time, they should always take periodic breaks. These breaks are needed to rest the mind, and often serve as good transition points between subjects. I recommend that children take a five- or ten-minute break during each hour, but they should schedule them so the activity does not become indiscriminate or excessive. During these breaks, youngsters should do something that is totally unrelated to school. They might play with a toy, do a chore, or just sit back and do nothing. Everyone needs a little time to goof off, and sometimes doing so can be a great refresher.

Even though children may study hard in the evening, they should try to avoid studying right up to the time they are ready to go to bed. This will only make them feel like they are on a treadmill. Children should take a little time at the end of the day to do some routine activities like brushing their teeth or getting their materials ready for school the next day. The time before bed is also a good occasion for parents to spend time with their youngsters, talking things over or reading a story. All parents should make time for these moments on a regular basis.

Good Habits

There are some basic habits that all of us should acquire, and it does not hurt to get children started early. Youngsters should be in good health if they are to reach their potential in their studies. They should always get plenty of rest, because they will not be able to think deeply or concentrate for an extended period of time if they are tired or rundown. Children should always eat three meals a day—yes, including breakfast—because they will lack energy if they are undernourished. Parents should also attempt to keep children away from junk foods, if possible, since they can have an adverse effect.

After spending so much time in a sedentary position at school, children will also need to have some physical activity to keep them mentally sharp. Just about all schools have programs in physical education, but it is wise to supplement these with extracurricular sports, as long as they do not become too intense and time consuming. Regular physical activity increases mental performance. Like trained athletes, children need to be at the top of their form to compete.

Just as there are good habits to acquire there are plenty of bad habits to avoid. Parents should help their children avoid activities that waste an excessive amount of time. As I have already mentioned, good examples of time-wasters are watching television and playing video games. These are superficial activities that do not develop any real talent or skill, yet American children spend far more time on them than on their studies. Parents need to put a firm limit on how many minutes their children can spend on these activities each day. All children need a little entertainment, but this will force them to select things that they really want to do rather than blindly sitting in front of the television set all day. Some children also waste an excessive amount of time playing with their friends. All youngsters need to play, but don't let it get in the way of studying.

Everyone seems to feel that they cannot accomplish as much as they would like each day, but this is so because they do not make efficient use of their time. Even young children can benefit from practicing the principles of time management. As a first step in helping your children to become more proficient in their use of time, have them take a close look at their activities during a typical school week. Teach them how to determine when they were making the best and worst uses of their time. Identify occasions when they accomplished a lot, and other instances that they wasted altogether. This will help them pinpoint inefficiencies in their schedule so they can modify their behavior to correct the situation. I realize that people—especially children—cannot change their lifestyle overnight, but they can at least make some minor modifications that will put them on the right track. Using time efficiently will help children feel that there are many more hours in the day to do other things they like.

Just as it is a bad habit to study too little, it is also a bad habit to study too much. In order to have a normal childhood, children need plenty of time to play and develop naturally. They should never become so obsessed with their studies that they neglect their physical and mental well-being. Children who spend all of their time cooped up with their studies are missing a part of their lives that they can never recapture. Their goal should be to do enough work to make top grades in all of their studies, and then go out and do all of the other things that give them pleasure. The beauty of the system I have presented here is that I tell students what they need to do to reach the top, and the rest of the time is their own. Many older students have told me that this enables them to enjoy their leisure time more fully, because they do not have to worry about whether they have done "enough" in their studies. They have plenty of self-confidence that they will succeed, and are able to enjoy "leisure with dignity."

Developing the proper study habits makes studying much easier and more enjoyable for children. Parents who help their youngsters become more proficient in their studies will also find that it makes their own task of helping their children much easier and more enjoyable.

Principle 1
Parents should help their children develop the proper study habits, so they can become top-notch students and still have time left over for other things.

2

Conclusion

In this book I have covered everything I know about how parents can help their children become top-notch students. I have shown you how to set the stage from the earliest years so children will be prepared to learn once they get into school. I have explained how you can help your youngsters master the Three R's: reading, writing, and arithmetic. And I have described how you can help children follow a comprehensive system that will enable them to get the most from their studies, prepare for assignments, study for tests, and obtain top grades. Moreover, I have presented several tips that will help children develop the proper study habits that will bring big dividends not only now, but well into the future.

With a knowledge of all of this material, can you now expect your child to become a top-notch student? The answer is that it is not that simple—much more is required.

Thomas Fuller, the English writer, said that "Knowledge is a treasure, but practice is the key to it." The most important thing children need to do to make this system work for them is to follow it. They are not going to become excellent students just because they understand everything in this book. They need to practice each of the steps I have outlined in every class throughout the entire year. If they do anything else, they are not really following my system and will not get the best results from it. I know this to be true from my own experiences, the experiences of my children, and those of the many students who have followed my system in the past. Most students do not have the discipline and the willpower to follow everything I have described here. Those who have followed it completely realize the greatest success, while those who have been halfhearted derive only part of the gain.

Not only will children have to follow my system, they will have to work very, very hard to realize their goals. My system shows them how to "work smart," but this does not relieve them of the workload. In any line of business, including school, hard work is the only true road to success. As Thomas Edison said, "Genius is one percent inspiration and ninety-nine percent perspiration."

What will it take for your children to work this hard? The main factor is that they must be highly motivated. When children are motivated they are interested in what they are doing, recognize its importance, and have the ambition to work hard to realize their goals. They are not deterred by obstacles or temporary setbacks; they strive for excellence no matter how difficult the situation. One advantage is that as children become more adept in their studies, this usually motivates them to do even better in school.

Many children have difficulty becoming motivated, because they think they would rather be doing something else rather than go to school. The best advice to give them is that they might as well work hard and make school a high-quality effort because they have to be there for a certain amount of time anyway. Also tell them that it is wise to put forth their best effort in school at an early age because this will help them get into the right college and ultimately, the occupation of their choice. Make sure that children know what is involved in gaining access to certain occupations. For example, to become a doctor you have to have very good grades in school, graduate from college, go to medical school, be an intern, and so forth. Whatever field to which your child aspires, emphasize that all of this work is worthwhile because a good occupation brings a lifetime of enjoyment, considerable earnings, and perhaps a certain amount of prestige as well. Even small children are motivated by such factors.

Children also need to realize that even if they work very hard, they should not expect to accomplish everything at once. Few people become top-notch students overnight. It may take a while, and plenty of practice, to refine the study skills I have presented. Part of growing up is learning how to deal with disappointments. I tell older students to "expect miracles from my system but not perfection." Even if younger students follow my system to the letter, they will probably have some disappointments until they perfect the techniques. As I have said earlier, we all make mistakes, and the main thing is to learn from them so we do not repeat the same errors over and over again.

I am confident that children following my study system will experience amazing progress right from the outset. They should derive additional satisfaction as they move closer to their goal and see their grades improve. Moreover, if they are following my system carefully they will prevail in the long run, because they are on the right track. The whole learning experience will become more enjoyable because it is a natural human tendency to take pleasure from something when one is good at it. As I have discovered with my own children, they enjoy getting good grades in school, and they will not settle for a mark that they feel is beneath them. After a while, youngsters do those things naturally that are required of hard-working students, learning becomes easier, and good grades are a by-product.

What can you and your children expect from all of the effort in school? Reseachers have found that people who do well in school are more likely to be successful in other areas of their lives. While they are in school, they are more likely to have friends, participate in extracurricular activities, and even hold school offices. These are some of the factors that make for a happy childhood. Moreover, they are more likely to be successful after they get out of school as well, if good jobs, high salaries, and personal recognition are any indication. For these are the things that make for a happy adulthood.

I have seen the methods presented here work wonders for my own children, and I am happy to share them with the parents of other children. I know that these methods would have made my life much easier and more enjoyable when I was a young student, if I had been aware of them then. Now that you have read this book, your children can take advantage of these methods *now* and become top-notch students.

More than twenty-five hundred years ago, the ancient Chinese sage Lao Tzu said, "A journey of a thousand miles must begin with a single step." You have taken the first step by reading this book. The rest of the journey will be up to you and your children. Godspeed.

Principle 2
Parents can help their children become top-notch students by making sure that they know what they are doing, work hard, and have confidence of success.

SUMMARY

Part Four
Making the System Work for Your Child

PRINCIPLE 1
Parents should help their children develop the proper study habits, so they can become top-notch students and still have time left over for other things.

PRINCIPLE 2
Parents can help their children become top-notch students by making sure that they know what they are doing, work hard, and have confidence of success.

References

Adler, Mortimer J., and Charles Van Doren. *How to Read a Book*. New York: Simon and Schuster, 1972.

Armstrong, William H., and M. Willard Lampe, II. *Study Tips*. New York: Barron's Educational Series, Inc., 1983.

Black, Ginger E. *Making the Grade*. New York: Carol Publishing Group, 1989.

Carnegie, Dale. *How to Win Friends & Influence People*, revised edition. New York: Simon and Schuster, 1981.

Cohn, Marvin. *Helping Your Teen-Age Student*. New York: E. P. Dutton, 1979.

Doman, Glenn. *How to Teach Your Baby to Read*. New York: M. Evans & Company, Inc., 1990.

Eastman, Peggy, and John L. Barr. *Your Child is Smarter Than You Think*. New York: William Morrow and Company, Inc., 1985.

Flesch, Rudolph. *Why Johnny Can't Read*. New York: Harper & Row Publishers, 1955.

Gould, Toni S. *Get Ready to Read*. New York: Walker and Company, 1988.

Graves, Ruth, ed. *The RIF Guide to Encouraging Young Readers*. New York: Doubleday & Company, Inc., 1987.

Green, Gordon W., Jr. *Como Sacar una A*, Spanish translation of *Getting Straight A's*. New York: Carol Publishing Group, 1992.

_____. *Getting Ahead at Work*. New York: Carol Publishing Group, 1989.

_____. *Getting Straight A's*, revised and updated edition. New York: Carol Publishing Group, 1993.

_____. *Math Made Simple* (for elementary and junior-high-school students). New York: Carol Publishing Group, forthcoming.

McKeown, Pamela. *Reading*. London: Routledge & Kegan Paul, 1974.

Mitchell, William. *The Power of Positive Students*. New York: William Morrow and Company, Inc., 1985.

Rich, Dorothy. *Megaskills*. Boston: Houghton Mifflin Company, 1988.

Trelease, Jim. *The Read-Aloud Handbook*. New York: Penguin Books, 1979.

Appendix A
Multiplication Table

	1	2	3	4	5	6	7	8	9	10	11	12
1	1	2	3	4	5	6	7	8	9	10	11	12
2	2	4	6	8	10	12	14	16	18	20	22	24
3	3	6	9	12	15	18	21	24	27	30	33	36
4	4	8	12	16	20	24	28	32	36	40	44	48
5	5	10	15	20	25	30	35	40	45	50	55	60
6	6	12	18	24	30	36	42	48	54	60	66	72
7	7	14	21	28	35	42	49	56	63	70	77	84
8	8	16	24	32	40	48	56	64	72	80	88	96
9	9	18	27	36	45	54	63	72	81	90	99	108
10	10	20	30	40	50	60	70	80	90	100	110	120
11	11	22	33	44	55	66	77	88	99	110	121	132
12	12	24	36	48	60	72	84	96	108	120	132	144

Appendix B
Key Words Used
in Examinations*

Key Terms of Quantity, Duration, or Degree

All, always	Necessarily	—any exception
Only	Necessary	makes these
Without exception	Never	statements false
	No, None	
Rarely	Almost always	—imply a judgment
Seldom, Infrequent(ly)	Usual(ly), Often,	of frequency or
Occasional(ly)	Frequent(ly)	probability
Some, Sometimes	Probably	
Few	Many	
Several	Most	
About, Around	Approximate(ly)	

Descriptive and Analysis Questions

Describe, Review   —give account of the attributes of
                        the subject under discussion
                        (inherent characteristics, qualities)

Discuss   —tell all you know about the subject
                        that is relevant to the questions
                        under consideration

*As printed in Grassick, *Making the Grade*, Arco Publishing, Inc., New York, 1983. This material was originally adapted from Jason Millman and Walter Pauk, *How to Take Tests*, McGraw-Hill, New York, 1969.

State	—briefly "describe" with minimal elaboration
Analyze	—separate the subject into parts and examine the elements of which it is composed
Enumerate, List, Tabulate	—briefly present the sequence of elements constituting the whole
Develop	—from a given starting point, evolve a logical pattern leading to a valid conclusion
Trace	—in narrative form, describe the progress, development, or historical events related to a specific topic from some point of time to a stated conclusion
Outline, Summarize	—give the theme and main points of the subject in concise form
Diagram, Sketch	—outline the principal *distinguishing* features of an object or process using a clearly labeled diagram

Explanation and Proof Questions

Explain, Interpret	—state the subject in simpler, more explicit terms
Define, Formulate	—classify the subject; specify its unique qualities and characteristics
Prove, Justify, Show that	—demonstrate validity by test, argument, or evidence
Demonstrate	—explain or prove by use of significant examples
Illustrate	—explain fully by means of diagram, charts, or concrete examples

Comparison Questions

Compare	—investigate and state the likeness or similarities of two or more subjects
Contrast	—look for noticeable differences
Relate	—establish the connection between one or more things

Personal Judgment Questions

Criticize, Evaluate	—judge or evaluate the subject for its truth, beauty, worth, or significance; and justify your evaluation. "Criticize" doesn't necessarily mean a hostile attack—it is more a matter of comment on literal or implied meaning.
Interpret	—explain and evaluate in terms of your own knowledge
Justify	—ordinarily this implies that you justify a statement on the author's terms. When asked to justify your own statements, defend your position in detail and be convincing.

Problem/Solution Questions

Find Solve Calculate Determine Derive What is . . .?	—using the data provided (some of which may be irrelevant) apply mathematical procedures and the principles of formal logical analysis to find a specific quantity in specific units

About the Author

Gordon W. Green, Jr. knows a lot about education. He received an A in every graduate course he took en route to receiving a Ph.D. in economics from the George Washington University in 1984. This accomplishment was quite remarkable, considering that Dr. Green was attending graduate school part-time in the evening, working more than full-time at his regular job, and taking care of home and family responsibilities at the same time. Even with this busy schedule, he had plenty of time for leisure activities.

Dr. Green attributes his success to a unique system of study that he developed, which he first reported on in his book, *Getting Straight A's*. Since it was originally published in 1985, *Getting Straight A's* has been advertised numerous times in *Parade* magazine and has helped hundreds of thousands of students earn higher grades in school. In 1992, the work was translated into Spanish as *Como Sacar Una A*, and now enjoys distribution worldwide. In the present volume, *Helping Your Child to Learn*, Dr. Green had adapted his study methods to the needs of elementary and junior-high-school students.

Dr. Green is now chief of the Governments Division at the U.S. Bureau of the Census. He directs the preparation of financial and employment statistics for federal, state, and local governments across the country, as well as a wide variety of statistics on elementary, secondary, and postsecondary education, and the criminal justice system. Before that, he was an assistant chief in the Housing and Household Economic Statistics Division at the Bureau of the Census, where he directed the preparation of the nation's official statistics on income distribution and poverty. His Ph.D. dissertation on wage differentials for job entrants received national attention, including a front-page article in *The New York Times*, articles in several other newspapers and magazines, and he appeared on national television to discuss his findings. His work is widely published in government periodicals, magazines, and professional journals.

Advice for Parents - Fun For Kids
Books For Children & Families From Carol Publishing Group

Ask for the books listed below at your bookstore. Or to order direct from the publisher call 1-800-447-BOOK (MasterCard or Visa) or send a check or money order for the books purchased (plus $3.00 shipping and handling for the first book ordered and 50¢ for each additional book) to Carol Publishing Group, 120 Enterprise Avenue, Dept. 1497, Secaucus, NJ 07094.

Autistic Children: A Guide for Parents and Professionals by Lorna Wing, M.D., D.P.M. paperback $7.95 (#50294)

Children's Letters to Santa Claus, Compiled by Bill Adler hardcover $9.95 (#72196)

Children's Letters to Socks: Kids Write to America's "First Cat," Edited by Bill Adler hardcover $9.95 (#72221)

Cults: What Parents Should Know by Joan Carol Ross, Ed.M. & Michael D. Lange, Ph.D. paperback $5.95 (#40511)

The Day Care Kit : A Parent's Guide to Finding Quality Child Care by Deborah Spaide paperback $7.95 (#72031)

Everything Your Kids Ever Wanted to Know About Dinosaurs & You Were Afraid They'd Ask by Teri Degler paperback $9.95 (#72096)

Getting Straight A's by Gordon W. Green, Jr., Ph.D. paperback $9.95 (#40571)

Great Videos For Kids: A Parent's Guide to Choosing the Best by Catherine Cella paperback $ 7.95 (#51377)

How to be a Pregnant Father by Peter Mayle; illustrated by Arthur Robins paperback $8.95 (#40399)

Kids' Letters From Camp, Edited by Bill Adler hardcover $9.95 (#72226)

Kids Pick the Best Videos for Kids by Evan Levine paperback $9.95 (#51498)

Maybe You Know My Kid: A Parent's Guide to Identifying, Understanding and Helping Your Child With Attention Deficit Hyperactivity Disorder by Mary Fowler paperback $12.95 (#72209)

The *Reading Rainbow* Guide to Children's Books: The 101 Best Titles by Twila C. Liggett, Ph.D. and Cynthia Mayer Benfield; Introduction by LeVar Burton hardcover $19.95 (#72222) paperback $12.95 (#51493)

The Santa Claus Book by Alden Perkes paperback $14.95 (#40381)

Upside Down Tales: Two books in one— a classic children's tale, and an alternative, amusing version that sets the record straight!

Hansel & Gretel/The Witch's Story by Sheila Black; Illustrated by Arlene Klemushin paperback $8.95 (#51520)

Jack & The Beanstalk/The Beanstalk Incident by Tim Paulson; illustrated by Mark Corcoran paperback $8.95 (#51313)

Little Red Riding Hood/The Wolf's Tale by Della Rowland; Illustrated by Michael Montgomery paperback $8.95 (#51526)

The Untold Story of Cinderella by Russell Shorto; illustrated by T. Lewis paperback $8.95 (#51298)

"What Am I Doing in a Stepfamily?" by Claire Berman; illustrated by Dick Wilson paperback $8.95 (#40563)

"What's Happening to Me?" by Peter Mayle; illustrated by Arthur Robins paperback $8.95 (#40312)

"Where Did I Come From?" by Peter Mayle; illustrated by Arthur Robins paperback $8.95 (#40253)

"Why Am I Going to Hospital?" by Claire Ciliotta & Carole Livingston; illustrated by Dick Wilson paperback $8.95 (#40568)

"Why Was I Adopted?" by Carole Livingston; illustrated by Arthur Robins paperback $8.95 (#40400)

Winning Bedtime Battles: How to Help Your Child Develop Good Sleep Habits by Charles E. Schaefer, Ph.D. & Theresa Foy DiGeronimo, M.E.D. paperback $9.95 (#51318)

Zulu Fireside Tales: A Collection of Ancient Zulu Tales to be Read by Young and Old Alike by Phyllis Savory; illustrated by Sylvia Baxter paperback $9.95 (#51380)

Prices subject to change; books subject to availability